THE GREAT
G.O.A.T. DEBATE

THE GREAT
G.O.A.T. DEBATE

The Best of the Best
in Everything from
Sports to Science

Paul Volponi

ROWMAN & LITTLEFIELD
Lanham • Boulder • New York • London

Published by Rowman & Littlefield
An imprint of The Rowman & Littlefield Publishing Group, Inc.
4501 Forbes Boulevard, Suite 200, Lanham, Maryland 20706
www.rowman.com

86-90 Paul Street, London EC2A 4NE

British Library Cataloguing in Publication Information Available

Library of Congress Cataloging-in-Publication Data

Names: Volponi, Paul, author.
Title: The great G.O.A.T. debate : the best of the best in everything from sports to science / Paul Volponi.
Description: Lanham : Rowman & Littlefield, [2022] | Includes bibliographical references and index. | Summary: "This book will expand the horizons of teen and pre-teen readers in an exciting and engaging way, by debating the Greatest of All Time in a variety of categories. Topics include the greatest athlete of all time, greatest band, greatest inventor, greatest scientist, greatest writer, greatest sci-fi franchise, and more"—Provided by publisher.
Identifiers: LCCN 2021023894 (print) | LCCN 2021023895 (ebook) | ISBN 9781538153154 (cloth) | ISBN 9781538153161 (epub)
Subjects: LCSH: Handbooks, vade-mecums, etc. | Popular culture—Miscellanea. | Sports—Miscellanea. | Arts—Miscellanea. | History—Miscellanea. | Biography.
Classification: LCC AG106 .V65 2022 (print) | LCC AG106 (ebook) | DDC 031.02—dc23
LC record available at https://lccn.loc.gov/2021023894
LC ebook record available at https://lccn.loc.gov/2021023895

♾™ The paper used in this publication meets the minimum requirements of American National Standard for Information Sciences—Permanence of Paper for Printed Library Materials, ANSI/NISO Z39.48-1992.

"If there's a book that you want to read, but it hasn't been written yet, then you must write it."

—*Toni Morrison*

CONTENTS

INTRODUCTION

It doesn't matter what your passion is. It might be sports, music, books, art, movies, TV, video games, or any of a thousand other pursuits. During your lifetime, you will certainly encounter someone else who shares that same intense interest. And when you do, you'll probably begin to compare notes and talk about why that particular subject has captured you. Other voices will undoubtedly join in the conversation. Soon, a singular question will arise about that subject—who is the greatest of all time? The G.O.A.T., if you will.

That's when the spirited debate will start. Is Michael Jordan or LeBron James the greatest basketball player of all time? Is *Star Wars* or *Star Trek* the greatest sci-fi franchise? Are the Beatles or the Rolling Stones the greatest band? Is Nas or Jay-Z the greatest hip-hop artist? Is Voldermort or the Joker the greatest villain? Of course, there are other worthy subjects too. Such as who is the greatest scientist of all time: Albert Einstein or Marie Curie? Who is the greatest orator (public speaker): Martin Luther King Jr. or Sir Winston Churchill? Who is the greatest philosopher, chess player, writer, inventor, or electric guitar player?

You may have come to this book to focus on a few subject areas in which you already have a strong interest. But while you're here, be sure to read several of the other categories as well. In doing so, you'll open new doors of knowledge. You'll learn things that will impress your friends, family, teachers, and most importantly, yourself.

Along the way, we will introduce you to some basic debating techniques. Those techniques will not only help strengthen your arguments as to who is the G.O.A.T. in each category, but also they will improve your ability to voice your opinion on any subject. You will also encounter some fun *lightning debates*—tongue-in-cheek, mini-arguments meant to make you think and smile. So let *The Great G.O.A.T. Debates* begin. It's time to form your own conclusions as to who is the greatest of all time.

We understand that the pair of participants we've picked to debate about in each category may not be the entries that you would have chosen. Here's the truth: we're not any smarter than you. So if you believe that you have a better entry, one that you think is more deserving, then speak up. Tell everyone you know. Formulate an argument and perhaps write a new entry to rival ours. We're absolutely interested in your opinions.

ATHLETE (ALL AROUND)

Mildred "Babe" Didrikson Zaharias vs. Jim Thorpe

Who is the greatest athlete of all time? That's an incredibly interesting debate. Why? Training methods, nutrition, and dozens of other important factors have vastly improved throughout the years, making comparisons of athletes from different eras a rather difficult argument. So we've chosen a pair of deserving and superversatile athletes—a male and female—from roughly similar time periods. The debate floor is yours.

MILDRED "BABE" DIDRIKSON ZAHARIAS (1911–1956)

> *"The formula for success is simple: practice and concentration, then more practice and more concentration."* —M. B. Z.

She was given the name "Babe" after hitting five home runs in a childhood baseball game by friends who compared her to baseball great Babe Ruth.[1] Not an outrageous comparison considering Mildred "Babe" Zaharias would grow up to become perhaps the most talented woman athlete to ever compete in sports.

Born in Port Arthur, Texas, Babe Zaharias excelled at track and field, basketball, baseball, and golf. "All of my life I have always had the urge to do things better than anybody else," said Zaharias. "Before I was ever in my teens, I knew exactly what I wanted to be when I grew up. My goal was to be the greatest athlete that ever lived."[2]

Coming out of high school in the late 1920s, an era when there were no college athletic scholarships for females, Texas-based employers were more than eager to hire Babe. Not because she was an expert seamstress, but so that she could play on their company athletic teams. It was a form of local advertising back then—for a company to own a championship squad in a particular sport, with their company name splashed across the jersey.

Babe, though, aspired to higher competition. At the National AAU (Amateur Athletics Union) Track and Field Championships, Zaharias finished first in six separate events. That earned her a spot on the US Olympic Team and a trip to the 1932 Summer Olympics in Los Angeles, setting the stage for this Texas athletic legend to become an international hero.

Zaharias broke four world records during the games—two in the 80 meter hurdles, and one each in the javelin and high-jump. She won a pair of gold medals and a silver medal, becoming the only woman to ever win medals in running, throwing, and jumping events.

At the age of twenty-four, Babe began to play golf. Though she came to the sport late in life, Zaharias excelled at an exceedingly high level. She competed against men in a sanctioned pro event. Only four other women have ever attempted that. "Golf is a game of coordination, rhythm, and grace; women have these to a high degree," noted Zaharias.

After winning female championship events in both the United States and England as an amateur, Zaharias turned pro in 1947 and dominated the women's circuit, becoming the Ladies Professional Golf Association (LGPA) leading money-winner in 1950 and 1951.

Babe Zaharias planned on playing golf until she was into her nineties, even if that meant hitting a golf ball from a rocking chair. Sadly, she passed away at fifty-six, her life taken by colon cancer. During her final years, Babe became an advocate for the American Cancer Society, using her fame to raise funds for future research.

Jim Thorpe Stamp.

**Mildred "Babe" Didrikson
Zaharias stamp.**

JIM THORPE (1887–1953)

He could simply do it all, seemingly without effort. Having never high-jumped before, a teenage Jim Thorpe watched the track and field team practicing at his Carlisle, Pennsylvania, school. He walked up to the bar and easily out-jumped everyone there while wearing his street clothes.

Thorpe was born in the Indian Territories of the West (now Oklahoma). He was a Native American, a member of the Sac and Fox Nation. With his parents deceased, he relocated east where athletics became his passion. At the 1912 Olympics in Stockholm, Sweden, Thorpe won gold medals in both the pentathlon (comprised of five events) and decathlon (comprised of ten events). He was the first Native American to win gold for the United States.

"I was never content unless I was trying my skill . . . or testing my endurance," said Thorpe. "[But] I am no more proud of my career as an athlete than I am of the fact that I am a direct descendant of that noble warrior [Chief Black Hawk]."[3]

Six months after his Olympic triumphs, a newspaper story appeared stating that Thorpe had played minor league baseball one summer, receiving approximately $2 per day for expenses. Unlike many other athletes who also participated in pro or semipro sports to support themselves, Thorpe hadn't played under an assumed name.[4]

The AAU, perhaps in prejudicial opposition to Thorpe's Native heritage, stripped him of his Olympic medals.

In a letter to the AAU, Thorpe wrote, "I hope I will be partly excused by the fact that I was simply an Indian schoolboy and did not know about such things. In fact, I did not know that I was doing wrong, because I was doing what I knew several other college men had done, except that they did not use their own names."[5]

His honesty only helped to seal his fate.

John "Chief" Myers, Thorpe's baseball roommate and fellow Native American, recalled, "Jim was very proud of the great things he'd done. A very proud man . . . Very late one night Jim came in and woke me up. . . . He was crying, and tears were rolling down his cheeks. 'You know, Chief,' he said, 'the King of Sweden gave me those trophies, he gave them to me. But they took them away from me. They're mine, Chief; I won them fair and square.' It broke his heart and he never really recovered."[6]

With his loss of amateur status, Thorpe went on to play professional baseball for six seasons. He then played pro football, winning three NFL Championships before there was ever a Super Bowl. Finally, this incredible athlete began a career in basketball, barnstorming around the country with a team comprised completely of Native Americans.

During the later stages of his life, Thorpe struggled with severe alcoholism. In poverty, he died of heart failure at the age of sixty-five.

In 1982, the International Olympic Committee agreed to posthumously return Jim Thorpe's medals to his surviving family members. The town of Jim Thorpe, Pennsylvania, is named in his honor.

TIME TO DEBATE

Perhaps you can approach your physical education teacher or coach and ask, "Who's the greatest athlete of all time?" When you receive an answer, make sure they explain their reasoning behind it. That's an essential part of any debate, presenting clear and concise reasons for your opinion.

Debater #1: "Babe Zaharias was an individual champion at several sports."

Debater #2: "Jim Thorpe won team championships in different sports, making the other athletes around him better."

Here's a quartet of incredible all-around athletes that might get you thinking about furthering this debate:

Jackie Joyner-Kersee: A three-time Olympic gold medal winner. She twice succeeded in the long-jump and once in the heptathlon (seven separate events).

Carl Lewis: Winner of nine Olympic gold medals for running, long jumping, and relays.

Jim Brown: All-time great at both football and lacrosse.

Bo Jackson: All-Star baseball and football player. His commercial tagline is "Bo Knows Sports."

THE GENUINE ARTICLE

Recently, a pair of professional sports teams has undergone name changes. Football's Washington Redskins and baseball's Cleveland Indians both finally agreed to rename their franchises. Native Americans had long complained that those team nicknames marginalized Natives, reducing them to mere mascots in the eyes of the public. But during the 1922 and 1923 pro football seasons, Jim Thorpe was the player/coach for a team completely comprised of Native Americans. They were called the Oorang Indians and played their home games in Marion, Ohio. Their roster included players named Arrowhead, Big Bear, Black Bear, Dear Slayer, Joe Little Twig, Red Foot, Red Fox, and Wrinkle Meat.

2

BAND (MUSIC)

The Beatles vs. Rolling Stones

Bands are unique to the art of music. Unlike individual performers, their success depends on a collective synergy between band members. Do they complement each other's talents? Can they make the individual sacrifices needed to survive as a unit? Or are they destined to break up? Who's the greatest band of all time? In many people's opinions, there are really only two choices.

THE BEATLES

George, Paul, John, and Ringo—that's all you need to say and people will immediately know that you're speaking about the English rock band the Beatles. The group was formed in Liverpool, a metropolitan city in the UK, in 1960. Just four years later, they had hit the shores of the United States and vaulted themselves to international stardom, even beyond the scope of popular music. The Beatles influenced fashion with their style of dress (black collarless suits) and banged haircuts, as well as contributing to a youthful revolution in society often referred to as the "counterculture" movement.

"The basic thing in my mind was that for all our success, the Beatles were always a great little band. Nothing more, nothing less," said Paul McCartney. "I think that, particularly in the old days, the spirit of the Beatles seemed to suggest something very hopeful and youthful."[1]

The four-piece band, consisting of John and George on guitar, Paul on bass, and Ringo on drums, played packed stadiums across the United States. When the Beatles made their first national TV appearance on the *Ed Sullivan Show* (at the time a top-rated variety program), seventy-three million people watched them perform.

As the group toured the United States, it took a stand against the south's policy of racial segregation by refusing to play in cities and stadiums where Blacks were not allowed to occupy the same seating areas as whites. The Beatles were so popular during this time period that some southern cities bent to the band's desires, holding their first nonsegregated concerts.

The Beatles were recognized for great songwriting, led by the writing team of John Lennon and Paul McCartney, who coauthored many of the band's biggest hits including "All You Need Is Love," "Come Together," "A Day in the Life," "Hey Jude," and "Let It Be."

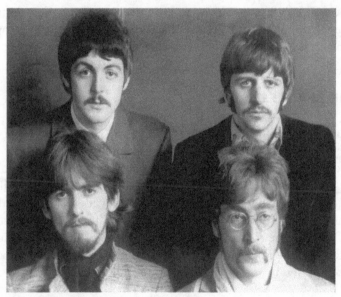

The Beatles. *Photofest © Photofest.*

"I'd spent five hours that morning trying to write a song that was meaningful and good, and I finally gave up and lay down. Then, *Nowhere Man* came, words (*He's a real nowhere man sitting in his nowhere land, making all his nowhere plans for nobody*) and music, the whole damn thing, as I lay down," said John Lennon. "Songwriting is about getting the demon out of me. It's like being possessed. You try to go to sleep, but the song won't let you. So you have to get up and make it into something, and then you're allowed sleep."[2]

Between 1964 and 1970, the Beatles changed both their musical style and appearance several times. Their sound ranged from pop to ballads to rock to a period of psychedelic music—all critically acclaimed and successful. They went from dressing in suits, to wearing Nehru jackets from India, to embracing a long-haired, unshaven hippy look.

When the Beatles broke up in 1970, it was major news. Each member continued to have musical success on their own. A Beatles reunion was something the press continuously speculated about until John Lennon was shot and killed by a deranged fan on the streets of New York City in 1980. The band was inducted into the Rock & Roll Hall of Fame in 1988, and each of the four members was later inducted individually for their solo careers.

ROLLING STONES

The Rolling Stones have been recording music and filling concert venues worldwide since 1962. That's more than half a century. Their charismatic lead singer, Mick Jagger, is one of rock and roll's most iconic figures and an extraordinary stage presence. The band was formed in England by founding member Brian Jones, who named the group after a song by famed bluesman Muddy Waters titled "Rolling Stone." Much of the Stones' sound was influenced by the great US blues players of the 1940s and 1950s including Robert Johnson, Lightnin' Hopkins, Bo Diddley, Chuck Berry, Howlin' Wolf, Lead Belly, and Muddy Watters.[3]

Like the Beatles, the Rolling Stones were introduced to a US audience on the *Ed Sullivan Show* in 1964. But they were subjected to censorship in performing their hit "Let's Spend the Night Together."

The chorus was deemed too sexual for TV. Mick Jagger was forced to instead sing the lyric, "Let's spend some *time* together."

Mick Jagger and guitarist Keith Richards, who were childhood friends, became the Rolling Stones' driving force and main songwriting duo after Brian Jones was booted from the band in 1969 because of his excessive drug use. Jones died a short time later, drowning in his swimming pool.

Ever since 1970, the Rolling Stones have been introduced on stage as "The greatest rock and roll band in the world." Their list of hit songs includes "Satisfaction," "Paint It Black," "Under My Thumb," "Sympathy for the Devil," "Wild Horses," and "Beast of Burden."

"People love talking about when they were young and heard (one of our songs) for the first time. It's quite a heavy load to carry on your shoulders, the memories of so many people," said Mick Jagger.[4]

Keith Richards, one of the world's most recognizable guitar players, has his own take on writing songs that have become part of popular culture.

"What is it that makes you want to write songs? In a way you want to stretch yourself into other people's hearts," said Richards. "You want to plant yourself there, or at least get a resonance, where other people become a bigger instrument than the one you're playing. It becomes almost an obsession to touch other people. To write a song that is remembered and taken to heart is a connection, a touching of bases."[5]

In 1981, while touring the United States, the Stones were in Chicago to play a series of concerts. They went down to a small blues club where their idol, Muddy Waters, was playing. Soon the band found itself on stage playing beside the man who was responsible for giving the Rolling Stones their name.

Other longtime members of the Stones are guitarist Ronnie Wood, drummer Charlie Watts, and bass player Bill Wyman. The band's logo is a pair of huge red lips with a tongue sticking out, resembling Mick Jagger.

In 2011, the band Maroon 5, featuring an appearance by singer Christina Aguilera, released a song called "Moves Like Jagger," in homage to Mick Jagger's dynamic on-stage dance moves.

Will the Rolling Stones ever retire?

"We age not by holding on to youth, but by letting ourselves grow and embracing whatever youthful parts remain," said Keith Richards. "[Besides] why would you want to be anything else if you're Mick Jagger?"[6]

TIME TO DEBATE

Debates are special. Why? They can provide us with the opportunity to accomplish two things: Voice our personal opinions, and solve a problem or dispute. Our dispute for the moment is simply to determine who is the greatest band of all time—The Beatles or the Rolling Stones? When you provide an answer to that question, it's called your "position." That's the place where you stand on a certain issue.

Debater #1: "The Beatles are the greatest band of all time because they caused a musical revolution with their style and sound."

Debater #2: "The G.O.A.T among bands is the Rolling Stones because of their incredible longevity."

Hopefully, after our band debate has concluded, your opinion and position will help us settle upon an answer.

LIGHTNING DEBATE

Here's an opportunity for you to quickly debate a fun topic: Your favorite band has rented the house next door in which to rehearse. It's well after midnight and they're still playing really loudly. (Free concert right?) Only you have an early morning final exam at school the next day and need to sleep. So you get out of bed and knock on their door. Do you tell them to turn it down or do you ask to be invited inside?

THE BIG SCREEN

Both the Beatles and Rolling Stones have been part of several films. The Beatles appeared in *Help!*, *Yellow Submarine* (animated), and *A Hard Day's Night*. Meanwhile the Stones rocked the big screen in *Gimme Shelter* and *Sympathy for the Devil*. There's even a recent film titled *Yesterday* (2019), which imagines a world where the Beatles never existed. But perhaps the best film ever made about the inner workings and inspiration behind a band is *Straight Outta Compton*, directed by F. Gary Gray. The film details the 1986 bonding of Eazy-E, Dr. Dre, Ice Cube, DJ Yella, and MC Ren in their formation of the band N.W.A. The film is hailed for its raw, no-holds-barred depiction of how life on the streets of Compton, California, inspired and influenced a group of five aspiring artists.

BASEBALL PLAYER

Babe Ruth vs. Hank Aaron

Who is the greatest of all time among baseball players? That's a debate fans have participated in for generations. Is a pitcher more valuable than a batter? Are an abundance of base hits more valuable than home runs, which are hit in fewer numbers? And how do we judge modern-day stars such as Mike Trout, Albert Pujols, Aaron Judge, Mookie Betts, and Clayton Kershaw against their counterparts from past eras? Well, that's half the fun of the debate—believing we each know the correct answer. By the way, one of our two participants below was both an all-time great hitter and pitcher. Play ball!

BABE RUTH (1895–1948)

> *"Never let the fear of striking out keep you from coming up to bat."*
> —G. H. R.

Nicknames are something that can follow athletes throughout their careers. Baseball star George Herman Ruth, better known to the world as "Babe," seemed to collect nicknames the way he hit home runs—in big numbers. He was called "Babe" because of his reputation as a promising young player. Ruth was also referred to as "The

Bambino" and the "Sultan of Swat" (for being the home run king). In fact, Yankee Stadium was nicknamed after him, called "The House That Ruth Built."

Growing up as a youngster on the streets of Baltimore, though, Ruth had a different type of reputation. He was branded a juvenile delinquent, unable to be controlled by his parents, who eventually sent him to a reform school—St. Mary's Industrial School for Boys.

Babe Ruth. *Photofest © Photofest.*

There, Ruth studied shirt-making and carpentry. However, fate had a different road chosen for the athlete who was destined to revive baseball from relative obscurity, elevating it to the nation's most popular sport through his immense talent and larger-than-life persona.

Sold to the New York Yankees from the Boston Red Sox, where he'd helped his former team capture a trio of World Series titles, Ruth lead the Yanks to four future championships. Meanwhile, the Red Sox, suffering from the so-called Curse of the Bambino, didn't win another title for eighty-six years.

Ruth and the city of New York were a perfect combination. The abundance of media there helped to make him a legendary hero: he would promise sick kids in hospitals he'd hit home runs for them, and then delivered on his word. He even earned a higher salary than the US president. When asked by the press about it, Ruth reportedly replied, "I know, but I had a better year than (Herbert) Hoover."[1]

While playing during the "dead-ball era," when baseballs didn't fly out of ballparks with regularity, Ruth routinely hit more home runs himself than entire opposing teams during a season.

"I swing as hard as I can, and I try to swing through the ball. The harder you grip the bat, the more you can swing it through the ball, and the farther the ball will go. I swing big, with everything I've got. I hit big or I miss big. I like to live as big as I can," said Ruth.[2]

Babe Ruth ended his twenty-two-year playing career with a total of 714 home runs. At the time, it was the most ever hit. But he was also multitalented. As a starting pitcher, he won 94 games and lost only 46, a dominant winning percentage of .671 (top 10 all-time).

His teammate Waite Hoyt said of Ruth, "I've seen them—kids, men, women, worshippers—all hoping to get his name on a torn, dirty piece of paper. Or hoping for a grunt of recognition (by him) when they said, 'Hi-ya, Babe.' He never let them down, not once. He was the greatest crowd pleaser of them all."[3]

HANK AARON (1934–2021)

Despite having hit seven fewer career home runs than Barry Bonds, most people consider Hank Aaron's total of 755 to be the legitimate all-time home run mark in Major League Baseball. That's because Bonds played during the game's "steroid-era" (1992–2006) when many achievements were artificially enhanced.

Aaron began his baseball career with the Negro League's Indianapolis Clowns in 1952, even though Jackie Robinson had broken the color barrier in baseball five years earlier by being the first African American in MLB.

Here's what Aaron wrote about his experience with the Clowns and racism after the team finished their morning meal in a Washington, DC, restaurant: "We had breakfast while we were waiting for the rain to stop, and I can still envision sitting with the Clowns in a restaurant behind Griffith Stadium and hearing them break all the plates in the kitchen after we finished eating. What a horrible sound. Even as a kid, the irony of it hit me. Here we were in the capital in the land of freedom and equality, and they had to destroy the plates that had touched the forks that had been in the mouths of Black men. If dogs had eaten off those plates, they'd have washed them."⁴

Born in Mobile, Alabama, Hank Aaron made his big league debut in 1954 with the Braves. Though he never hit more than 47 homers in a single season (Babe Ruth once hit 60), the Braves outfielder was an ultraconsistent slugger hitting 30 or more home runs fifteen times during his remarkable twenty-three-year career.

Hank Aaron didn't have a typical slugger's physique. Unlike Ruth, who stood 6-foot-2 and weighed almost 220 pounds, Aaron was just 6-foot and 180. Though he didn't possess bulky muscles, Aaron had extremely powerful wrists, which added extra pop to his bat.

As the 1974 season began, Aaron was just one home run shy of Ruth's magical 714 record. The slugger, as well as several reporters giving him positive press, received death threats and an avalanche of hate mail from those who didn't want to see a Black man surpass Babe Ruth. But on his very first swing of the 1974 season, Aaron homered in Cincinnati, tying Ruth at 714. Four days later, with the Braves playing in Atlanta before a packed stadium of hometown fans, Aaron stepped to the plate in the fourth-inning of the nationally televised game.

"He's sitting on 714. Here's the pitch . . . Swinging. There's a drive into left-center field. That ball is gonna be-eee . . . Outta here! It's gone! It's 715! There's a new home run champion of all time, and it's

Hank Aaron. *Photofest © Photofest.*

SWEET SWING

The Baby Ruth candy bar, which made its debut in 1920, was named after baseball great Babe Ruth. However, the Curtis Candy Company initially denied it. Most believe that was done in an effort not to compensate Ruth financially for the use of his name. Well, the candy maker eventually did strike a settlement with the baseball great, ending the charade.[5]

Fast forward to 1978, when the Curtis Candy Company unveiled their new Reggie Bar, named after Yankees' slugger Reggie Jackson. This time the candy maker compensated the player up front, and even put his picture on the wrapper.

On opening day, the company gave every fan to enter Yankee Stadium a free Reggie Bar. It worked out great until Jackson hit a home run early in the game and the fans littered the field with candy bars in appreciation, causing a prolonged and rather messy stoppage in play.

Henry Aaron! The fireworks are going. Henry Aaron is coming around third. His teammates are at home plate. And listen to this crowd!" said announcer Vin Scully. "What a marvelous moment for baseball. . . . What a marvelous moment for the country and the world. A Black man is getting a standing ovation in the Deep South for breaking a record of an all-time baseball idol. And it is a great moment for all of us, and particularly for Henry Aaron. . . . And for the first time in a long time, that poker face in Aaron shows the tremendous strain and relief of what it must have been like to live with for the past several months."

WHAT IS DEBATE?

Debate occurs when a particular topic is discussed, usually by more than one speaker, presenting different or opposing viewpoints. Debates can be formal—using rules and allotted times to speak—or they can be quite casual, such as a spirited conversation or argument between friends. Your school might even have a debate team. Members of the debate team, under the guidance of a coach or teacher, practice building and winning arguments against one another. The ultimate goal is usually to compete against other schools at a formal debate where judges listen to the arguments and ultimately declare a winner. The art of debate can trace its roots back to the philosophical and political debates of ancient Greece (twelfth to ninth centuries BC) and ancient India (2600 to 1300 BC). Plato, a Greek writer and philosopher, is often credited with refining the concepts of how to successfully advance an argument through debate.

You've probably seen debates on TV between political candidates. Major networks often carry the presidential and vice presidential debates because those are national offices. Regional TV stations carry mayoral or congressional debates for more localized elections.

So whenever you argue your points about who is the G.O.A.T. at something, you're actually participating in a longtime academic tradition of self-expression.

4

BUILDING DESIGNER/ARCHITECT

Zaha Hadid vs. Frank Lloyd Wright

Maybe you like to build and design things. You're into LEGO bricks. You glue toothpicks or Popsicle sticks together. Perhaps you're a student of the game Jenga or have a passion for erecting a multilevel house of cards. Well, that's basically what an architect does, only on a much bigger scale. They imagine, design, and then plan structures such as bridges, monuments, homes, office buildings, skyscrapers, and even stadiums—with their initial visions going from paper or a computer screen to real life.

Cities such as New York, Chicago, Toronto, Seattle, Paris, Hong Kong, and Sydney all have distinctive skylines. You may even know the names of some of the famous structures in those cities, and have their striking silhouettes committed to memory. But do you know the names of the people who designed them? Probably not. So we'll provide you two celebrated names in the field to begin the potential debate: Who's the greatest architect of all time?

ZAHA HADID (1950–2014)

In an occupation dominated by men, Zaha Hadid broke the glass ceiling. Her gravity-defying designs and use of geometric shapes to create eye-catching structures earned her a reputation as the "Queen of Curves." Hadid, who was born in Baghdad, Iraq, and trained in London, also had a passion for painting. That greatly influenced her architecture. "The whole idea of lightness, floating, structure and how it lands gently on the ground: It all comes from [my study of painters]," said Hadid, who is known for her ability to bend concrete and glass into natural-looking forms.[1]

For the 2012 Summer Olympics held in London, Hadid designed the Aquatics Center, which hosted all of the swimming events. Moved by the natural shape of water in motion, Hadid was inspired to create a roof for the structure that rises up like an ocean wave. Nature was also Hadid's inspiration for creating the highway bridge that connects Abu Dhabi Island (in the United Arab Emirates) to the southern Gulf shore. The bridge's roadway, which stretches a half-mile, gently rises and falls mirroring the region's many sand dunes.

"There are 360 degrees. So why stick to one?" said Hadid of her designs. "Architecture is really about well-being. I think that people want to feel good in a space. . . . On one hand, it's about shelter, but it's also about pleasure."[2]

FRANK LLOYD WRIGHT (1867–1959)

Widely recognized as the greatest architect in American history, Frank Lloyd Wright designed over a thousand structures and had a career that spanned more than seventy years. He is especially known for his organic style of architecture, using natural elements like stone and wood. Among his most famous structures is a rural Pennsylvania home called Fallingwater, which is built over a waterfall. The multi-level house has a pair of terraces that blend into the natural rock formations and appear to float over the downward-streaming water. Wright didn't want the family living there to simply look out over the fall. "[I wanted them] to live with the waterfall . . . as an integral part of their lives," said Wright.[3]

Perhaps Wright's most famous structure is New York City's Guggenheim Museum. Its seashell-like interior and circular design took Wright sixteen years and over two hundred sketches to go from inception to

Fallingwater house in Mill Run, PA, designed by Frank Lloyd Wright. *Public Broadcasting Service (PBS)/Photofest © Public Broadcasting Service (PBS).*

completion.[4] Visitors are encouraged to take an elevator to the top and view the museum's artwork as they slowly descend a sweeping spiral ramp. Its organic design changed the way society envisioned museums, making them seem less stuffy and formal. Unfortunately, Wright died six months before his masterpiece of design opened to the public.

"Study nature, love nature, stay close to nature. It will never fail you," said Wright of his organic sense of structure. "Buildings too are children of Earth and Sun."[5]

TIME TO DEBATE

Who do you think is the G.O.A.T. when it comes to architecture— Zaha Hadid or Frank Lloyd Wright?

Most of us have a lot of experience at arguing a particular side, whether we're asking our parents for a larger spending allowance or a later curfew. Or perhaps lobbying our teachers for a higher grade on an exam or assignment. So don't be intimidated by the word "debate." Most good arguments are like well-written essays. They have a clear thesis statement or singular, well-focused point to present. See our examples below:

Debater #1: "I think Zaha Hadid is the G.O.A.T. because of her ability to bend glass and concrete as if they were natural elements."

Debater #2: "The G.O.A.T. of architects is absolutely Frank Lloyd Wright because his nature-inspired designs are admired worldwide."

Of course, there are other great architects who could also vie for this title. Here are five names and structures they've designed. Perhaps you'll research them a bit and then present your own argument in their favor.

Jeanne Gang—Conceived the design of Chicago's 82-story Aqua Tower.

Santiago Calatrava—Designed the Olympic Sports Complex of Athens.

Stephen Sauvestre—The main architect of the Eiffel Tower in Paris.

John Graham—Imagined Seattle's flying saucer–shaped Space Needle.

Ustad Ahma—This seventeenth-century architect is credited with designing both the Taj Mahal and the Red Fort at Delhi.

PILING ON

If you're a budding architect, we have a game especially for you. Jenga is a building game designed by Leslie Scott. Players take turns removing one block at a time from a tower consisting of fifty-four blocks. The removed blocks are then placed on top of the tower, creating a progressively taller and more unstable structure. The name Jenga comes from a Swahili (a language of the African Great Lakes region) word meaning "to build."[6] Since making its debut in 1982, Jenga has sold over eighty million games. Perhaps the game's G.O.A.T. is Robert Grebler of California, who in 1985 built the tallest known tower consisting of 40⅔ levels. Will you outdo him one day?

5

CHESS PLAYER
Hou Yifan vs. Garry Kasparov

It should absolutely be an equal playing field between men and women when it comes to competing at chess. But that hasn't been the reality. There have been few women to occupy a slot among the top-ranked players in the world. Why? Women simply haven't had the same opportunities as men to study beneath a great chess master or compete against the highest-quality competition on a consistent basis. We urge you to read Walter Tevis's novel *The Queen's Gambit*, about a coming-of-age female chess player. Netflix recently released a miniseries of the same name based on the book. Our debate on who is the G.O.A.T. of the squared black and white board will take that uneven male/female equation into consideration as we pit a chess queen against a chess king. Choose your side!

HOU YIFAN (B. 1994)

> *"There are two different personalities. Some players only see chess, but others see chess in all things—beauty, fashion, strategy. I'm clearly the second type."* —H. Y.

One of the hardest parts about being a chess champion is budgeting your time. True greatness requires many hours a day of intensive study. Most of the memorable champions of the past gave up on having any type of life outside of chess. The common thinking is: if you don't dedicate all of your free time to the game, you'll be at a distinct disadvantage against other world-class players. Now, enter a young champion with a different point of view. She is Hou Yifan, a Chinese chess grand master and multiple-time Women's World Chess Champion. In 2012, against the advice of her chess coach, Hou enrolled in Peking University to study international relations. "I want to be the best [at chess]," said Hou. "But you also have to have a life."[1] In school, she took full class-loads and participated in a wide variety of extracurricular activities. Upon graduation she was offered a Rhodes Scholarship to begin her graduate work at Oxford University in England. How serious is she about living a diverse life? Hou basically surrendered her world championship by missing tournaments to pursue other goals that were important to her.

Hou Yifan learned to play chess at three and has been studying to play at a high level since she was six. By age sixteen, she'd won her first Women's World Championship. "I've had full family support," said Hou, who has been traveling to tournaments with her mother from the start. "My mom decided to pause her (career) to accompany me. She really helped me a lot with my series of chess achievements. . . . If you have full concentration and inspiration you should play chess. . . . Not (because) your parents want you to play. . . . Don't give up your daily life. . . . Keep chess as one of your (many) interests."[2]

At age twenty-six, Hou was appointed as a professor at Shenzhen University, in their School of Physical Education. How did that happen? A chess player with a degree in international relations named as a professor of physical education? Well, in China, chess isn't considered a game. It is an official sport. Of course, Hou will help to coach students there who aspire to play at a championship level. But she also believes that chess can be very important to the personal growth of even the casual player. "[I hope] to use chess to help organize the overall ability of students and cultivate their innovative thinking," said Hou.[3]

GARRY KASPAROV (B. 1963)

"The loss of my childhood was the price for becoming the youngest world champion in history." —G. K.

The word "aggressive" is usually reserved for football players, boxers, and martial artists; not chess masters. But aggressive is the only appropriate way to describe the style of play of chess champion Garry Kasparov. His boldest moves have best been exhibited in the opening stages of a match where Kasparov is intent on gaining an edge against his opponent. "If you wish to succeed, you must brave the risk of failure," noted Kasparov of his style.[4] Combined with his incredible capacity to study the board and ability to adjust tactics to the changing flow of a game, Kasparov has a substantial claim on being considered the G.O.A.T. of the squared board. Indeed, Garry Kasparov, born in the Soviet Union, held the title of World Chess Champion from 1985 (the youngest ever at the age of twenty-two) to 2000.

Kasparov has been a participant in several famous chess matches. Just prior to winning his first title, Kasparov battled against then-champion Anatoly Karpov in a match that lasted five months before it was declared a draw by officials due to "exhaustion" on the part of both players. Kasparov, however, learned valuable lessons from that experience, and the very next year, he was crowned champion.[5] He is also one of the co-subjects of perhaps the best book ever written on chess. It is titled *The Longest Game: The Five Kasparov/Karpov Matches for the World Chess Championship*, authored by Jan Timman, a Dutch chess grand master. How bold is Kasparov? In 1997, Kasparov took on an IBM supercomputer named Deep Blue in a much publicized chess match, only to be defeated by the machine.

"Chess helps you to concentrate, improve your logic. It teaches you to play by the rules and take responsibility for your actions, how to problem solve in an uncertain environment," said Kasparov. "Solving new problems is what keeps us moving forward as individuals and as a society, so don't back down."[6]

Kasparov has been bold in his life outside of chess as well. As a political activist and chairman for the Human Rights Foundation, he has spoken out many times about the lack of freedom for the Russian people beneath the dictator-like rule of Russian President Vladimir Putin. Accordingly, Kasparov's website was banned from being viewed there, and his chess accomplishments were removed from some Russian record books. For his own safety, Kasparov no longer lives in Russia. Since 2014, he has resided in Croatia with no regrets over his political actions.[7]

"Regret is a negative emotion that inhibits the optimism required to take on new challenges. You risk living in an alternative universe, where if only you had done this or that differently, things would be better. That's a poor substitute for making your actual life better, or improving the lives of others. Regret briefly, analyze and understand, and then move on, improving the only life you have."[8]

TIME TO DEBATE

One of the keys to being a successful debater lies in your ability to anticipate a counterargument—what your opponent will present as the problems or flaws in your own argument—and to state why your opponent is wrong. For example, if you choose Hou Yifan as the G.O.A.T. among chess players, it will undoubtedly be brought up that she was never World Champion, only the Woman's World Champion. See how our pair of debaters below deals with that.

Student Debater #1: "Maybe Kasparov has accomplished more as a chess champion but, as a woman, Hou Yifan has risen to an incredible height with far less opportunity."

Student Debater #2: "Because of the historic lack of high-level training for women chess players, it's hard to support the notion that Hou Yifan could even be considered the G.O.A.T."

WITH THE EYES OF THE WORLD WATCHING

A chess match getting the same type of publicity as the Super Bowl or World Series? Well, that's exactly what happened in 1972, at the World Chess Championship in Iceland, when the United States's Bobby Fischer took on the USSR's Boris Spassky to vie for the crown. Why did it capture the world's attention? The two participants represented superpower countries that were archrivals in the Cold War (a war played out in other ways than on the actual battlefield). Many observers believed that that chess match was the equal to the United States and Russia battling each other for world supremacy. Despite the Soviets' domination of chess for several decades, Fischer of the United States defeated Spassky. The 2014 film *Pawn Sacrifice*, starring Tobey Maguire of *Spider-Man* fame, is based on the events surrounding that 1972 match.

6

COMPOSER

John Williams vs. Ludwig van Beethoven

Musical pieces spring from the minds and talents of composers. Their job is to arrange the notes to create a desired melody, mood, and dynamic. When they hit on something magical—an arrangement that totally captures an audience's attention—it's hard to deny. It sticks in listeners' brains as they tap their toes to the rhythm, possibly singing or humming along. Who is the greatest composer of all time? It's a really tough debate to stage because people favor different types of music. There's classical, modern, pop, jazz, folk, rock, reggae, country, ska, and many more. So we've chosen a pair of composers who have been recognized by a rather wide audience for their musical compositions.

JOHN WILLIAMS (B. 1932)

John Williams plays the piano and trombone. Only those aren't the talents for which he's known throughout the world. It really doesn't matter what language you speak, Williams communicates to an audience through his music. And though you might not be familiar with his name, you are very likely to instantly recognize his work.

Williams has composed the musical scores for some of the most important and popular movies ever made. These films include *Star Wars*, *Jaws*, *Superman*, *Raiders of the Lost Ark*, *E.T. the Extraterrestrial*, *Harry Potter and the Sorcerer's Stone*, *Return of the Jedi*, and *Saving Private Ryan*.

The son of a jazz drummer, Williams began his professional musical career playing piano in New York City jazz clubs. After moving to Los Angeles, he started getting work writing music for TV shows. Soon filmmakers called upon Williams's talent to compose movie scores.

Stephen Spielberg asked Williams to create the music for *Close Encounters of the Third Kind*, a film in which aliens could only communicate with us through music—a composer's dream job.

Spielberg then recommended Williams to his friend George Lucas, who needed a score for his upcoming film *Star Wars*. Williams created the personal themes for several characters, including the uplifting music to accompany Luke Skywalker, as well as the tense percussion and horn-laden Imperial March for Darth Vader.

"You never write a theme for a movie thinking, 'This will live forever,'" mused Williams. "[But] there are occasionally eureka moments. Off the top of my head, maybe Darth Vader's theme. You know, the Imperial March."[1]

Williams is also responsible for ratcheting up the tension in the movie *Jaws*. He created the signature music for the arrival of the mammoth great white shark with a series of notes, mimicking a rapidly increasing heartbeat—*bum-bump-bum-bump, bum-bump-bum-bump*.

For Spielberg's *Jurassic Park*, Williams had a dual job—portraying both the stature and raw power of the dinosaurs. Williams described the gentle opening theme as being meant "to capture the awesome beauty and sublimity of the dinosaurs in nature." Later, when the moods of these immense creatures change, the composer uses a large orchestra to mirror their swift and powerful "rhythmic gyrations."

How does Williams feel about composing music which has thrilled audiences for generations?

"So much of what we do is ephemeral [short-lived] and quickly forgotten, even by ourselves. So it's gratifying to have something you have done linger in people's memories," noted the composer.[2]

LUDWIG VAN BEETHOVEN (1770–1827)

*"To play a wrong note is insignificant; to play without passion is
inexcusable!"* —L.V.B.

There's a reason the character Schroeder from *Peanuts* has a small
bust of the German-born Ludwig van Beethoven on his piano. The
youngster is among the many musicians who consider Beethoven—an
otherworldly talent and someone completely dedicated to music—as
their hero. That's quite the recognition when you consider that during
the middle stages of his life, Beethoven, who was considered a vir-
tuoso pianist, began to suffer increasingly from deafness. Yes, perhaps
the greatest composer of all time continued to create masterpieces of
music despite a loss of hearing. Beethoven actually used to bite down
upon an iron rod connected to his piano soundboard. That allowed
the composer to feel the vibrations coming from his piano, and, in his
mind, translate those vibrations into sound.[3]

Beethoven's music speaks to us without words. It walks in concert
with the human spirit, emulating life with its power, drive, and passion.
Those feelings can certainly be experienced in just the opening notes of
Beethoven's famous Fifth Symphony—*dun-dun-dun-dunnn! dun-dun-
dun-dunnn!* You've undoubtedly heard this suspenseful and tempo-
building opening as the background to many films and commercials.

"I would rather write 10,000 [musical] notes than a single letter of
the alphabet," asserted the composer.[4]

The Fifth Symphony is written in the key of C minor, giving it a
stormy and unsettling feel, as if an ever-increasing wind might rip
the roof from the listener's house. The piece has become one of the
cornerstones of classical music and is probably the most played by
symphony orchestras around the world.

Music was Beethoven's life and unequaled passion. During his
workaholic career as a composer, he wrote a staggering nine sym-
phonies, seven concertos, seventeen string quartets, thirty-two piano
sonatas, ten violin sonatas (instrument solo), five cello sonatas, one
sonata for the French horn, and an opera titled *Fidelio*.

When he died, the composer's headstone had only one word etched
into it, "Beethoven." That's how recognizable his name is in society.

TIME TO DEBATE

Using images and emotions in your argument are a good way to succeed in a debate. Try to connect to similar feelings shared and experienced by others. That's exactly what our two composers do. They
connect to the listener by creating music that conjures feelings and
emotions, making the listener an active participant.

*Student Debater #1: "The heroic music that plays in the background
when Luke Skywalker first steps onto the screen makes us want to root
for him. The way John Williams accomplishes that is an amazing feat."*

*Student Debater #2: "Beethoven's Fifth Symphony makes us want
to jump up and put our bodies into motion. It gets our blood pumping.
I know I'm not the only one who feels that way. It's a gift Beethoven
has given the world."*

Neither of our two composers wrote lyrics to go with their music.
But modern songwriters, who are also composers of music, usually do
and are recognized as some of our most celebrated poets. Here are
a few names of prolific songwriters, just in case you want to research
them and formulate a different debate: Paul Simon, Adele, Lady
Gaga, Carole King, Kendrick Lamar, Eminem, Tupac Shakur, Otis
Redding, Townes Van Zandt, Marvin Gaye, Aretha Franklin, Chuck
Berry, Leonard Cohen, and Bob Dylan.

LIGHTNING DEBATE

Let's say songstress Taylor Swift and Ludwig van Beethoven lived
during the same time period and had dated. Which one of the two
do you believe would have written the better song about their high-
profile breakup?

7

DANCER (FEMALE), DANCER (MALE)

Anna Pavlova vs. Janet Jackson,
Mikhail Baryshnikov vs. Michael Jackson

In the category of female dancer, there are many gifted artists from which to choose. Ultimately, we decided to stage a battle of "old school" vs. "new school" for the purposes of our debate. So take a spin around the dance floor with each of our entries. Then come to your own conclusion about who is the G.O.A.T.

ANNA PAVLOVA (1881–1931)

Unless you're a serious student of dance history, you may have never heard of Anna Pavlova. But she was considered to be the best dancer in the world at the very beginning of the twentieth century, a time when there was no TV or internet to trumpet her talents into every household.

Anna's story is one of great sacrifice, all in the name of her life's consuming passion to dance. Born prematurely in the city of St. Petersburg (part of the then Russian Empire), Anna Pavlova was smallish, thin, and sickly as a child. At the age of eight, she saw a performance of a ballet called *The Sleeping Beauty* and was mesmerized by it. Just one year later, Anna tried out for the famed

Imperial Ballet School but was rejected. She didn't allow that initial disappointment, though, to derail her dream. After another year of intense practice, she was finally accepted by the school through a subsequent audition. Only that wasn't the end of difficult times for Anna. Her classmates made fun of her thin body, referring to her as "The Broom." She even needed to reinforce her ballet slipper with leather and small pieces of wood because the arches of her feet never developed properly.[1] This also resulted in ridicule from her peers. But Anna kept practicing, especially on her own outside of class. Of her inner drive to become the best, Anna said, "No one can arrive from being talented alone. God gives talent, work transforms talent into genius."[2] And after many years of intensive work, Anna became the prima ballerina (number-one dancer) at the school. Her most famous dance was called the *Dying Swan* in which she interpreted the movements of a bird's final moments.

Eventually, Anna Pavlova became so popular that she was able to start her own dance company, keeping total creative control over every aspect of her art. She traveled extensively, drawing substantial crowds to every performance, and became one of the most well-known entertainers in the world. How committed was Anna to the art of dance? While touring Europe in 1931, at the age of forty-nine, she contracted a terrible case of pneumonia. Her doctors said that she needed surgery to recover. But the twist was that the surgery would rob her of the ability to continue dancing. Anna refused the operation, declaring, "If I can't dance, I'd rather be dead!" A short time later, while at the threshold at death's door, Anna instructed her caretakers to "Get my swan costume ready." Not long after, she passed away.[3]

You can see Anna Pavlova dance the Dying Swan *on YouTube.*

JANET JACKSON (B. 1966)

When it came time to choose a "new school" artist in our debate for the G.O.A.T. of the dance floor, it became much easier when several of our other possible choices, including Jennifer Lopez, Paula Abdul, Beyoncé, Britney Spears, and Lady Gaga, identified Janet Jackson as someone who was a major influence on their style. Janet Jackson is an accomplished singer, songwriter, and actress. But among her peers, she's most widely recognized for her contributions as a dancer. Born in Gary, Indiana, Jackson is youngest of ten children in a clan that comprised the Motown musical group the Jackson Five, featuring the singing and dancing talents of her brother Michael Jackson. Janet started performing with the group when she was just seven years old. Though we've tagged her as "new school," Jackson was influenced in both her music videos and concert stage shows by "old school" dancers such as Fred Astaire, who made a huge impact on dance in film, and Michael Kidd, who did the same while choreographing (designing dance movements) Broadway productions.

Other performers sought out the choreographers that Jackson had working relationships with, hoping for similar results. "The funny thing is, they really had no idea how hard it is to do what [Janet] does,"

CONTROVERSIAL PERFORMANCES

Janet Jackson's career has not been without controversy. At the 2004 Super Bowl in Houston, Texas, while performing at halftime with Justin Timberlake, Jackson had an "oops" moment. Part of her costume tore away, briefly exposing her bare breast to more than 143 million viewers and causing a public outcry. The incident brought a new phrase into our lexicon: "wardrobe malfunction." That moment led to a widespread debate over perceived indecency in public broadcasting, as well as a slew of large fines from the FCC (Federal Communications Commission). Some called it a publicity stunt because of the massive attention Jackson received. She denied it. "It's truly embarrassing for me to know that [over 140 million] people saw my breast, and then to see it blown up on the internet the size of a computer screen," said Jackson. "But there are much worse things in the world (war, famine, HIV) for this to be such a focus. I don't understand." Many media outlets around the country, for a period of time, blacklisted Janet Jackson's music and videos in retaliation. The "oops" moment led to a five-second delay on many live telecasts, so networks can censor unexpected content. Many media experts have also conjectured that the overwhelming number of viewers who wanted to see the replay of Jackson's mishap eventually inspired the creation of YouTube.

said choreographer Tina Landon, who worked with Jackson on several iconic projects.[4] Known for her precise steps, often redefining standard moves to give them her own signature flair and intensity, Jackson and her world-class team of backup dancers have thrilled audiences worldwide. "I don't believe in luck," said Jackson on delivering incredible performances. "It's persistence, hard work, and not forgetting about your dream." So it's fitting that her dream to dance has inspired so many others to do the same. "I believe in a higher power. I believe in inspiration," added Jackson.[5]

Whom would you choose as the greatest female dancer of all time, Anna Pavlova or Janet Jackson? Naturally, we realize there are many other forms of dance besides ballet and modern/hip-hop. Maybe you have a different genre of dance in mind? One with its own iconic star. So the larger debate is now open between you and anyone else with an opinion and a passion for dance.

DANCER (MALE)

Selecting the greatest male dancer of all time is not an easy task. There are so many genres of dance—jazz, Latin, modern, ballroom, swing, jive, country, Irish step dance, and Cajun, just to name a few. Each one proudly boasts a dance master of its own. So for our debate, we decided to focus on two very different types of dancers: one is very genre-specific while the other mixed several genres together, uniquely forming his own style. Those participants are ballet's Mikhail Baryshnikov and dance innovator Michael Jackson.

MIKHAIL BARYSHNIKOV (B. 1948)

Mikhail "Misha" Baryshnikov was born in Latvia, a republic held tightly under control by the oppressive U.S.S.R. (Russian) regime. Baryshnikov's father was a very strict military officer. His mother, though, had a passion for the arts and introduced her son to dance. Sadly, Baryshnikov's mother committed suicide when he was just twelve years old. That same year, he seriously began to study ballet.

Mikhail Baryshnikov. *Cannon Films/Photofest © Cannon Films.*

Not long into his training, Baryshnikov displayed great promise and was considered among the top young dancers in a country where ballet was extremely prized. His main obstacle as a male ballet dancer was his height (5 foot 5). He wasn't offered starring roles because he wasn't taller than the ballerinas, and didn't appear to command the stage. But Baryshnikov eventually changed everyone's perception of that by his incredible ability to communicate his passion and inner feelings through his performance.

"When a body moves, it's the most revealing thing. Dance for me a minute and I'll tell you who you are," said Baryshnikov. "The body cannot lie. You cannot be somebody else onstage, no matter how good of an actor or dancer or singer you are. When you open your arms, move your finger, the audience knows who you are, you know."[6]

Mikhail Baryshnikov seemed to have everything he wanted in life, except to be free of his government's oppressive control. Then, while touring with the Russian Ballet in Toronto, Canada, in 1974, Baryshnikov literally made his dash to freedom. After a performance, he left the theater with the rest of the dance troupe. Hundreds of fans were waiting outside for his autograph. That's when Baryshnikov began running down the street. The secret police (Russian KGB agents), there to keep watch over Baryshnikov and the others, lost sight of him in the crowd of people, many of whom were chasing him for his signature. Baryshnikov jumped into a waiting car, which was arranged in advance by friends, and defected (to forsake one nation for another because of its ideology) to Canada on the grounds of "artistic choice."[7]

"I was not extremely patriotic about Mother Russia. I played their game, pretending. You have to deal with, you know, party people, KGB. [All] horrifying," said Mikhail Baryshnikov.

Baryshnikov eventually became an American citizen and a lead dancer with the New York City Ballet. He toured and was celebrated all over the world, but could never return to Russia under the threat of being arrested.

Along with American tap dancer Gregory Hines, Baryshnikov starred in the 1985 film *White Nights*, in which dancing and freedom are the major themes.

MICHAEL JACKSON (1958–2009)

Also known as "The King of Pop," Michael Jackson began his entertainment career with his brothers singing and dancing in the Motown
group the Jackson Five. Michael sang lead vocals and they recorded
hits such as *Dancing Machine*, with their younger sister, Janet Jackson, eventually performing alongside them. When Michael went solo,
dancing became a huge part of his stardom. Jackson wasn't aligned
with a particular genre or style of dance. Instead, his own unique
abilities set the trends of what people wanted to see, especially with
the help of networks such as MTV, which gave his music/dance videos vast audiences. In 1983, Jackson unveiled the moonwalk. It was a
dance step that had been around for many years. Jackson, however,
perfected it through his extreme body control and meticulous eye for
details. The dance move took the world by storm as both professional
and amateur dancers alike tried to replicate it.[8]

"People ask me how I make music. I tell them I just step into it. It's
like stepping into a river and joining the flow. Every moment in the
river has its song," said Jackson. "To live is to be musical, starting with
the blood dancing in your veins. Everything living has a rhythm. Do
you feel your music?"[9]

Other iconic MJ dance moves include—the lean, robot, toe stand,
and pelvic thrust. None of those moves was invented by Jackson, but all
of them became closely associated with him because of his outstanding
presence and technique. His ability to turn and spin at an incredibly
high velocity has marveled audiences. Music videos such as *Billie Jean*,
Thriller, and *Beat It* pushed dance to the fore. Jackson didn't even call
his works videos. Rather, he referred to them as "films."[10]

Unfortunately, Michael Jackson died at the age of fifty, due to car-
diac arrest induced by acute drug intoxication.

TIME TO DEBATE

In arguing the cases of both our female and male dancers there is
a debate technique that could prove very powerful, and it revolves

around presenting an unforgettable story. Stories are great vehicles to capture people's attention and emotions. A superbly constructed story will keep the listener finely tuned to the debater's narrative, anticipating either a satisfying or heartfelt conclusion.

Debater #1: "Ana Pavlova was so dedicated to her craft that she would have rather lost her life than to never dance again. After she became sick and was told she had a choice between getting well or never dancing again she chose . . ."

Debater #2: "Imagine being so dedicated to dance that you leave your family and friends behind. That's what Mikhail Baryshnikov did in order to have the freedom to pursue his profession. As he was exiting a theater in Toronto after dancing, a car was secretly waiting a few blocks away. Suddenly, Baryshnikov took off running . . ."

Yes, our debate left out a wide array of incredible dancers. There's dancer/choreographer Alvin Ailey, Bollywood's Madhuri Dixit, and Michael Flatley (Lord of the Dance), all of whom have their own immense followings. Musicians such as James Brown, Jennifer Lopez, MC Hammer, Tina Turner, Usher, Chance the Rapper, and Justin Timberlake are all admired for their ability to dance. Film stars such as John Travolta and Patrick Swayze combined their dancing and acting prowess to create memorable roles. So we leave it to you to keep the dancing debate alive and research any of the names mentioned here with which you're not familiar. *Break a leg!*

8

ELECTRIC GUITAR PLAYER

Jimi Hendrix vs. B. B. King

Throughout history, there have been many great guitar players. After all, guitars or chordophones—instruments that create sound by strings being pressed against a fretboard—have been in wide use since they first appeared in Europe during the twelfth century. There's even a three-thousand-year-old stone carving of someone playing a simple chordophone in ancient Babylonia.[1] But when it comes to debating the greatest guitar player of all time, we're going to bypass the acoustic version and focus solely on the electric guitar, which was first developed in 1932.

JIMI HENDRIX (1942–1970)

> *"Sometimes you want to give up the guitar. You'll hate the guitar. But if you stick with it, you're gonna be rewarded."* —J. H.

A former paratrooper in the US military, Jimi Hendrix was an absolute force of nature with an electric guitar in his hands. Of course, he didn't only play with his hands. Besides playing the guitar behind his head and between his legs, Hendrix also used his teeth and feet.

Jimi Hendrix. *Photofest © Photofest.*

Born in Seattle, Washington, the left-handed-playing Hendrix made a huge impact on the music industry and his guitar-playing contemporaries at the time. That was despite having a career that spanned only four years, cut short due to an overdose of barbiturates. Hendrix was admired for his incredible technique, as well as his ability to fuse various genres of music together, such as blues, jazz, rock, and soul. His dynamic stage presence and colorful clothes only added fuel to the fire audiences felt, and occasionally, Hendrix would literally set fire to his guitar as the climax of a *hot* show. Innovations, such as his use of a wah-wah pedal and combining lead and rhythm guitar, were also part of Hendrix's musical genius. Playing at a near-sonic volume, his extreme amplification produced astral-quality feedback and roaring distortion, while his fingers made lightning runs up and down the scales.[2] In a very real way, Hendrix redefined the electric guitar in his own striking image. "My goal is to be one with the music. I just dedicate my whole life to this art," said Hendrix.[3]

On September 18, 1970, guitar great Eric Clapton, who was in awe of Hendrix's raw ability, was supposed to meet him in London to attend a concert together. Clapton had even purchased Hendrix a present for the occasion. "The night that he died I was supposed to meet him. . . . I brought with me a left-handed Stratocaster [guitar]. . . . I'd never seen one before and I was going to give it to him," said Clapton. "But we never got together. The next day, he was gone and I was left with that left-handed Stratocaster."[4]

Go to YouTube and checkout Jimi Hendrix's unique performance of the Star-Spangled Banner at Woodstock in 1969.

B. B. KING (1925–2015)

Unlike the sadly shortened career of Jimi Hendrix, guitar legend B. B. King played the blues for seventy years. Born on a Mississippi cotton plantation, King was first attracted to music while attending church as a child. The minister there played guitar during services and later taught the young King his first three chords on the fretboard.[5] By the age of sixteen, King was performing at local churches and developing a fan-base from playing on radio shows in Mississippi, Tennessee, and Arkansas. Over the next few years, King formed his own band and started to become widely recognized for his ability to improvise (not follow a set pattern of notes) on the guitar. "The blues was bleeding the same blood as me," said King. "I was born on a plantation and things weren't so good. We didn't have any money. I never thought of the word 'poor' till I got to be a man, but when you live in a house that you can always peek out of and see what kind of day it is, you're not doing so well."[6]

B. B. King. *Photofest © Photofest.*

B. B. King took his unique brand of the blues from small clubs scattered across the United States and Europe to the world's largest concert halls. He was a master of note selection and placement while playing lead guitar with a soft, warm tone.[7] It is a style that has influenced nearly every blues guitarist since. In selecting notes, he wanted quality over quantity. King's solos often appeared simple and uncomplicated to the untrained eye. But your ears won't be as easily deceived. They'll register King's one-of-a-kind tones and phrasing as he bends and shakes notes to create vibrato (a variation in pitch).

King's favorite guitar was named "Lucille," and he claimed that she would often sing for him during performances.[8] How did B. B. King's guitar get the name Lucille? In 1949, while in an Arkansas bar, King witnessed two men fighting over a woman named Lucille. Their brawl caused a fire that burned the bar down. King ran out to safety before realizing he'd left his Gibson guitar behind. King immediately ran back into the blaze, which ultimately killed the two men who'd fought, to rescue his instrument. "I named my guitar Lucille to remind me to never do a thing like that again," said King.[9]

So whom would you choose for the G.O.A.T of the electric guitar: Jimi Hendrix or B. B. King? There are several others who are considered among the best ever. They include Eric Clapton, whose miraculous guitar playing earned him the nickname "God"; Jimmy Page of the band Led Zeppelin; Slash of Guns N' Roses; blues guitarist Samuel Lightnin' Hopkins; and the clean technique-driven Eddie Van Halen. Some of the most notable women who shred on electric guitar are Bonnie Raitt, Annie Clark, and Lita Ford.

TIME TO DEBATE

Electric guitars can certainly be loud. Debaters shouldn't be. Yelling your opinion over someone else's isn't the way to win a debate. The best speakers remain calm and polite, and follow the rules of

AIR GUITAR

Have little musical ability? Don't worry. You too can make your mark on stage as a guitarist—*an air-guitarist.* Every August since 1996, the Air Guitar World Championships have been held in Oulu in northern Finland. The competition's motto: Make Air. Not War. It is truly a world competition with past champions hailing from the United States, New Zealand, Japan, Netherlands, UK, Finland, Russia, Germany, and France. As you may have guessed, the performer pretends to play an imaginary electric guitar to recorded music. There are pretend riffs and solos, which may include the whipping of hair or the performer's bopping head punctuating the bass line. The act of playing air guitar is often coupled with imaginary singing, or lip-synching.

The winner of the most recent Air Guitar World Championships was the United States's Rob Messel, who was introduced to air guitar while serving in the US military. He plays air guitar in character as "The Marquis," an eighteenth-century French aristocratic time traveler making a brief stop in the twenty-first century to thrill us with his polished style of pantomime.[10] Rob, I mean the Marquis, even made an appearance on the reality competition show *America's Got Talent.* Just so you clearly understand, his *real* talent is *faking* a talent.

engagement. However, speakers can modulate their voices, both louder and quieter, for effect. They might change their speech's rhythm or cadence when trying to emphasize a specific point. Changing your tone of voice can also make your argument more interesting to the listener, giving their ears something fresh on which to focus. So the next time you're asked to speak at length on a subject, experiment with your voice. Even dropping down to a near whisper (if it's quiet enough around you) can cause the listener to intently zero in on your words.

9

HOOPS STAR (FEMALE), HOOPS STAR (MALE)

Maya Moore vs. Ann Meyers, LeBron James vs. Michael Jordan

Over the past half-century, women's basketball has truly blossomed as a major sport. It has grown from a marginalized game which presented few opportunities for the great female players to a number of vibrant, high-profile, and socially powerful leagues in the United States, Europe, and Asia. Who's the G.O.A.T. among female hoops stars? Our debate will focus on a woman who helped to put female players on the map, as well as a woman who is currently helping to push the boundaries of the sport today.

MAYA MOORE (B. 1989)

There are many ways to define a winner, especially in a team sport such as basketball. For Missouri native Maya Moore, the term "winner" is something that follows her both on and off the basketball court. While still in high school, Moore earned the honor of being named the National Gatorade Player of the Year, a distinction which included all prep players, male and female. She received a scholarship to the University of Connecticut, a traditional women's basketball powerhouse. During her four-year career in the Nutmeg State,

Moore led the UConn Huskies to a pair of NCAA Championships, on both occasions sporting a 39–0 undefeated season. The team's overall record during Moore's tenure as a student/athlete was 140–6, all while she maintained a 3.7 GPA in her classes.

"Trying to fit my strengths with my teammates' strengths, utilizing everyone to the max, is really fun to watch and really a fun way to play," noted Moore. "[As for myself], I want to be one of those players who you watch on film and say, 'Where's the weakness?'"[1]

Selected first overall in the 2011 WNBA draft by the Minnesota Lynx, Moore help her team capture the championship that season. The celebrations in Minnesota didn't end there, though. Moore was an essential part of bringing the Lynx a trio of additional WNBA titles over the course of the next six years. The 6 foot 1 small forward was also part of the United States's gold medal victories in the 2012 London Olympics and the 2016 games Rio de Janeiro.

Basketball isn't Maya Moore's only concern in life. In early 2019, Moore announced that she would forgo the upcoming WNBA season to focus on family and her dream of entering the ministry. Then in 2020, she again decided to temporarily shelve her athletic career to become an advocate for criminal justice reform.

"When I stepped away two springs ago, I just really wanted to shift my priorities to be able to be more available and present to show up for things that I felt were mattering more than being a professional athlete," said Moore, who was an outspoken critic on the treatment of both George Floyd and Breonna Taylor. "I think our criminal justice system has two problems. We have systematic problems and we have people problems. So if the hearts of people are not about justice than any system you have won't work."[2]

ANN MEYERS (B. 1955)

Is it possible that the G.O.A.T among women basketball players stands just 5 foot 9? Though her coaches mostly played her at shooting guard, Ann Meyers, at one time or another in her career, competitively fielded all five positions on the court, including playing center.

That was the type of overall talent and fortitude she possessed for the game. A native of San Diego, California, Meyers was the first high school student to ever play for the US National Basketball Team. As a college recruit, she was in such high demand that universities changed the way they approached women's athletics. UCLA actually gave her a four-year athletic scholarship—the first ever offered to a female athlete by the school.

The current standard for playing a great game would be recording a "triple-double" on the stat sheet. That means the player amassed double-digits in points, assists, and rebounds in a single game. Well, how about a quadruple-"double," adding steals into the mix. Meyers registered the first quadruple-double in Division One history during a 1978 UCLA victory. Her stat-line for the game read 20 points, 14 rebounds, 10 assists, and 10 steals. That same season ended with Meyers delivering UCLA a Women's National Championship.

In 1980, Meyers made headlines when the NBA's Indiana Pacers offered her a $50,000 no-cut contract. A woman had never played in the NBA before against men. Only the salary aspect was a done-deal. Meyers still needed to make the team during an open three-day tryout.

"My tryout was received with a lot of hostility. It really took me by surprise," said Meyers. "[In many eyes], I was doing something that was not acceptable. I was surprised and a bit overwhelmed by the negativity. I was just doing something that I had done my whole life. . . . The media was not very kind. . . . It was difficult for everyone because it was a first and they didn't know how to deal with it."[3]

Post-tryout, Meyers was released by the Pacers. To this date, no woman has yet played in an official NBA game.

"I was not familiar with being turned down because I had been successful through sports. It was a great learning lesson," Meyers concluded.[4]

Ann Meyers played professionally for three seasons with the New Jersey Gems of the Women's Professional Basketball League (WPBL), the forerunner of today's WNBA. In 1993, Meyers was enshrined in the Naismith Memorial Basketball Hall of Fame. Currently, she is a vice president in the front office of both the NBA's Phoenix Suns and the WNBA's Phoenix Mercury.

HOOPS STAR (MALE)

Great basketball players come in all shapes and sizes. Wilt Chamberlain was 7 foot 1 and once scored a record 100 points in an NBA game. On the opposite end of the height spectrum, Nat Robinson, who stands a mere 5 foot 9 in comparison, is a three-time NBA Slam Dunk Champion. Included among the best B-ballers ever are Kobe Bryant, Kareem Abdul-Jabbar, Oscar Robinson, Larry Bird, Ervin "Magic" Johnson, "Pistol" Pete Maravich, and Julius "Dr. J" Erving. Who's the greatest basketball player of all time? The pair presented below is probably the most discussed and debated when it comes to that question.

LEBRON JAMES (B. 1984)

Perhaps there has never been more pressure placed on the shoulders of a basketball player than the heavy burden carried since an early age by LeBron James. An Ohio high school phenom, James was projected by pundits, scouts, and fans to be one of the greats before he ever graduated from prep school. He didn't disappoint anyone. James bypassed college and went straight from high school to the NBA. To add to the already intense pressure, the native of Akron, Ohio, was selected number one overall in the 2003 NBA draft by his home state Cleveland Cavaliers, a team that had never won a championship and looked to James as its savior.

Even as a teenager, the 6 foot 9, 250-pound James was a dominant physical presence against older, more experienced NBA players. James's ability to dribble toward the hoop with a full head of steam—with a football-style mentality—resembled a runaway freight train that could thunderously dunk a basketball under the threat of making would-be defenders part of his personal highlight reel.

A multiskilled athlete, James, who is often called "King James," can score, pass, play defense, and lead a team to victory. "I think, team first. It allows me to succeed, it allows my team to succeed," said LeBron James. "Ask me to play, I'll play. Ask me to shoot, I'll shoot. Ask me to pass, I'll pass. Ask me to steal, block out, sacrifice, lead,

LeBron James. *Lionsgate/Photofest © Lionsgate.*

dominate, anything. But it's not just what you ask of me. It's what I ask of myself."[5]

James left the Cavaliers and won a pair of NBA championships with the Miami Heat. Then he returned home and marched the Cavs to their first ever championship in 2016, turning Cleveland into "Believe-Land." In 2020, he captured another title with the Los Angeles Lakers, giving "King James" his fourth NBA crown.

"I hate letting my teammates down. I know I'm not going to make every shot. Sometimes I try to make the right play, and if it results in a loss, I feel awful. I don't feel awful because I have to answer questions about it. I feel awful in that locker room because I could have done something more to help my teammates win," noted James. "You can't be afraid to fail. It's the only way you succeed."[6]

On multiple occasions, James has been named NBA MVP, NBA Finals MVP, All-Star Game MVP, First Team All-NBA, and First Team Defense All-NBA. He is simply one of the greatest players to ever walk onto the hardwood, blacktop, asphalt, or anywhere else a hoop could conceivably hang upon a backboard.

MICHAEL JORDAN (B. 1963)

Basketball superstar Michael Jordan worked relentlessly to cement himself in the consciousness of his coaches, teammates, and opponents. Maybe that's because he was once taken too lightly as a player and cut from his high school's varsity team. Only that didn't stop Jordan from being recruited by the University of North Carolina. The Brooklyn-born native even scored the game-winning basket in the Tar Heels' 1982 NCAA Championship, before being drafted by the NBA's Chicago Bulls two seasons later.

"Some people want it to happen. Some wish it would happen. And others make it happen," said Jordan. "My attitude is that if you push me towards something that you think is a weakness, then I will turn that perceived weakness into a strength."[7]

As an NBA rookie, Jordan immediately became a fan favorite with his unique ability to score from all angles, including an array of dynamic high-flying moves and slam dunks. He won the NBA Dunk contest in both 1987 and 1988, adding to the commercial prowess of his Air Jordan sneakers manufactured by Nike.

From 1991 to 1993, Michael Jordan led the Bulls to three consecutive NBA titles. He won an Olympic gold medal in 1992 with the USA's "Dream Team" comprised predominantly of NBA All-Stars. Then, amid all the glory and commercial hype, MJ suddenly retired from the sport after the 1993 season in an attempt to become a Major League Baseball player. The move was fueled in part by the horrific carjacking murder of his father, James Jordan, who loved baseball. Michael Jordan went on to play minor league baseball with the Chicago White Sox organization, though he never made it to the Major Leagues.

He returned to the NBA in 1995. Just one season later, Jordan again led the Chicago Bulls to a second run of three consecutive championships from 1996 to 1998. That made Jordan's record in the NBA Finals an amazing 6-for-6, providing him a solid claim as the G.O.A.T of professional basketball. Yet Jordan has always recognized that losing is part of the game and personal growth.

"I've missed more than 9,000 shots in my career. I've lost almost 300 games. Twenty-six times, I've been trusted to take the game-winning shot and missed. I've failed over and over and over again in

Michael Jordan. *Photofest © Photofest.*

my life. And that is why I succeed," said MJ. "I can accept failure, everyone fails at something. But I can't accept not trying."[8]

Adding to his perfect record in championships, Jordan is a six-time NBA Finals MVP, a fourteen-time All-Star, a ten-time NBA Scoring Champion and five-time NBA MVP.

No wonder Gatorade's commercial catch-phrase during the 1990s was "I wanna be like Mike."

TIME TO DEBATE

One powerful tool in debate can be using statistics to either prove or bolster your argument, also called "your position." Our basketball debate to determine the female and male G.O.A.T. of the court is a perfect place to use stats.

Debater #1: *"Maya Moore won more overall championships than Ann Meyers in both college and the pros."*

Debater #2: *"Michael Jordan is a perfect 6-for-6 in the NBA Finals. That's something LeBron James can never match, no matter how many titles he eventually wins."*

Just remember, try not to overuse statistics. Stick to the most important ones. Don't make your argument only about the numbers. That can quickly confuse or even bore the listener. Never lose sight of the human element when presenting your position.

LIGHTNING DEBATE

While still in high school, Michael Jordan got cut from the varsity basketball team. Here's your chance to debate that coach's decision. Was it the most foolish move a basketball coach has ever made? Or did that coach ultimately instill a competitive fire in Jordan to succeed at the game of basketball?

10

INVENTOR

Leonardo da Vinci vs. Nikola Tesla

Without inventors, it's not hard to believe that we'd be, in part, living in the past. Almost everything you'll use today—clock, pencil, refrigerator, elevator, microwave oven—was invented by somebody. Since the late eighteenth century, inventors have been issued patents (a government license giving them credit for their invention). Most recently, the TV show *Shark Tank* has introduced us to many inventors trying to create a business opportunity from their ideas. Who's the greatest inventor of all time? Many candidates can lay claim to the title. The Wright Brothers designed the first powered aircraft. Ben Franklin discovered electricity, created bifocals, a stove for heating a room evenly, and even the rocking chair. Alexander Graham Bell invented the telephone and Galileo the telescope. For this uber-competitive category and debate, we've focused on a pair of renowned inventors who lived four centuries apart.

LEONARDO DA VINCI (1452–1519)

A man of many diverse talents, Leonardo da Vinci made an indelible in subjects such as painting, astronomy, anatomy, paleontology (the science of fossils, and past animals and plants) and, of course, as an inventor. In fact, many of Leonardo's inventions or sketches of futuristic devices have become important parts of our modern world. Da Vinci just didn't have an excellent idea or two. Rather, he had a notebook full of marvels, often centuries ahead of a society with the technology to support them. His name translates as Leonardo of the city of Vinci, which is located in Florence, Italy.

Da Vinci is credited with inventing our modern-day parachute. Consider this: Leonardo envisioned the idea of a parachute before we had aircraft of any kind. Previously, a few people had tried to develop devices based on a similar idea of slowing a gravity-driven fall from a great height. Leonardo's design, however, was much more sophisticated. So much so, that in the year 2000 a British skydiver actually built a chute from da Vinci's original sketch, proving that it worked.

Leonardo, inspired by the wings of birds, sketched designs for different types of flying machines as well. His ornithopter (*ornithology* is the study of birds) had flapping wings powered by a human's muscle energy. The earliest notion of a helicopter is also found in da Vinci's sketchbook. He called it an aerial screw because of the twisting motion of the wings/rotors above the pilot's head. It's strikingly similar to our modern helicopters. And though aviation experts don't believe a human could provide enough power to keep it airborne, da Vinci is widely credited with being the first to imagine vertical flight.[1]

The inventive brain of da Vinci was one of the first to imagine an underwater diving suit, including a helmet, goggles, and a tube through which to receive fresh oxygen. Leonardo also came up with the idea for an early version of a military tank, complete with armor, a cannon, and a place for someone to sit inside so that it could be "driven." The first working tank didn't appear in battle until over four hundred years later. Here's the thing about da Vinci's original tank design—experts believed it would be too heavy to move. Many speculate that the inventor purposely designed it this way, not wanting his sketch to fall into the hands of an evil despot who might build an army of tanks and become invincible.[2] Da Vinci was far ahead of the curve when it came to automation—robots performing the jobs of humans. He also developed the idea of a mechanical knight that could sit, stand, and move its arms. It's often referred to as "Leonardo's Robot."

NIKOLA TESLA (1856–1943)

You've probably heard of the Tesla, an electric car manufactured by the auto company of the same name. Well, the Tesla was named in honor of one of the greatest inventors the world has ever known, Serbian-American Nikola Tesla. He was the scientist who developed alternating current or AC, which most of the world uses today. How brilliant was Tesla? His AC current basically buried an invention of Thomas Edison's (the creator of the electric lightbulb) called direct current or DC. Edison even wanted to hire Tesla to fix the problems plaguing direct current. But Tesla's AC was simply superior for large-scale usage. Why? Alternating current reverses its direction many times per second, allowing it to satisfy greater needs, such as supplying power to an entire city.[3] The electric outlets in our homes today provide AC, while batteries mostly provide the DC power we use.

How about reusable and sustainable energy? Tesla was at the forefront of that frontier as well. When Nikola Tesla was a young boy, his uncle read him a story about Niagara Falls. In Tesla's mind, he began to equate the idea of falling water with power. In 1895, he helped to create the first hydroelectric power plant at Niagara Falls. That began the electrification of the world, using Tesla's alternating current.

Tesla was also instrumental in inventing remote control devices. He began with a model of a small boat that he could steer from the shore. That early technology has blossomed today, providing us with remotes that operate lights, radios, door locks, and, of course, the channels on our TV. So if you're a proud couch potato who would prefer not to get up to perform various tasks, you absolutely owe Nikola Tesla a debt of gratitude.

The idea of wireless technology was also something that fascinated Tesla. Even Guglielmo Marconi, who is often credited with inventing radio transmission, used technology from several of Tesla's wireless patents. In fact, Tesla practically envisioned the way our society communicates today, via cell phones, Internet, TV, and radio. He invented the Tesla coil, the first system that could wirelessly transmit electricity. His early coil, however, could only transmit over short distances.[4] Tesla even built a tower in Brooklyn, New York, as a transmitter

Nikola Tesla.

station. The Nikola Tesla Museum *currently* stands on that site as a testament to his accomplishments.

Despite being issued over three hundred patents during his lifetime, Tesla wasn't good at business and died practically penniless in a New York hotel. It was rumored over the years that Tesla, who had done work with X-rays, had invented a death ray, like the ones we see in the science fiction movies. Did anyone take that rumor seriously? Well, immediately after Tesla's death, the FBI descended on his hotel room and searched for any ideas or technology they didn't want falling into the wrong hands.[5]

TIME TO DEBATE

There's nothing wrong with taking an edge in a debate, and trying to gain an advantage over your opponent. One of the great debaters was our sixteenth president, Abraham Lincoln. During the 1858 senatorial (for the position of US senator) debates in Illinois, Lincoln went head-to-head in a series of debates with incumbent-senator Stephen A. Douglas, mostly over the issue of slavery. Lincoln, who stood 6 foot 4, wore a stovepipe hat to make him tower over his opponent even more. And though Lincoln was extremely educated, he purposely used a lot of common language during the debates to better connect with his audience of farmers and working-class listeners.

UNDERCOVER INVENTOR

Hedy Lamarr was a famous film actress from the 1930s through the 1950s. But she was also an undercover inventor. As the former wife of a foreign arms dealer, she had heard the conversations of many Nazi generals at the start of World War II. After escaping to the United States, her hatred of the Nazi regime caused her to secretly work to defeat them. Along with composer and pianist George Antheil, she invented a frequency-hopping signal that could not be tracked or jammed. This would allow US torpedoes, launched from submarines, to find their targets and sink the German forces.[6] The US Navy didn't use it, however, until several years after it was invented. Why the delay? I suppose it was hard for the top military minds to fathom that an actress and a pianist could contribute something technical to the war effort.

Turns out the man known as "Honest Abe" was pretty tricky when it came to debating.

Back to the idea of being an inventor. Perhaps you've invented something yourself. Maybe it's a homework assignment that can't be eaten by a dog? Or sweat socks that don't stink up a gym locker? Well, lots of schools have clubs dealing with entrepreneurship (the art of business). That would be good place to showcase your invention or idea, potentially receiving some constructive feedback.

II

JAZZ SOLOIST

Ella Fitzgerald vs. Miles Davis

A truly American form of music, jazz, originated in New Orleans in the late nineteenth century, with its earliest roots evolving from the seeds of the blues and ragtime. Jazz is built on the theory of improvisation, creating licks and riffs on the spur of the moment. And at the heart of jazz are its solos and soloists bringing the audience something new with each performance. Jazz often treats a song as a bare-bones skeleton on which to hang new sounds. It's not the destination that's ultimately important—songs are simply a vehicle. Instead, jazz centers on the trip, highlighting every new twist and turn in the musical road that wasn't there before and may never be again. For every time a jazz artist solos, it is in some sense an original statement that might never be duplicated. Who's the greatest jazz soloist of all time? It's a tough call. But we've isolated two of the best for you to debate.

ELLA FITZGERALD (1917–1996)

"The only thing better than singing is more singing." —E. F.

Newport News, Virginia, native Ella Fitzgerald is simply known as the "Queen of Jazz." She had the amazing ability to use her voice as an instrument, taking on a hornlike quality in a jazz technique referred to as "scat." That's making up nonsensible words on the spot and singing them in rhythm to the melody, while occasionally departing from the song to improvise solos of free-flowing syllables and sounds. *See examples of various jazz artists, including Fitzgerald, scatting on YouTube.*

Fitzgerald didn't find her way to stardom easily. In the early 1930s, after relocating to New York City, she sang on the streets of Harlem for tips. At seventeen, she appeared on an amateur night at the famed

Ella Fitzgerald. *Photofest © Photofest.*

Apollo Theater. After winning that competition, the singer was asked to join a working jazz band. Over the succeeding few years, she recorded several hit songs.

"Just don't give up trying to do what you really want to do. Where there is love and inspiration, I don't think you can go wrong," Fitzgerald noted of her journey.[1]

Audiences praised the sense of freedom and emotion in her voice. Fitzgerald had a purity of tone, as well as unique phrasing when she sang. Her natural timing allowed her to blend seamlessly with the other instruments in the band, creating an incredible unison between the vocals, percussion, horns, and strings.

"Everybody wants to know about my style and how it came about. It's no big secret. It's the way I feel," said Fitzgerald. "I'm very shy, and I shy away from people. But the moment I hit the stage, it's a different feeling I get nerve from somewhere. Maybe it's because it's something I love to do."[2]

Fitzgerald was a trailblazer for women in the music industry, being one of the first women to ever front for a major band. She was also one of the first female stars not to fit the mold as being modelesque (model-like) in appearance. Her ability broke through those narrow doors, helping women to be recognized for their talent, instead of a sexist body-type preference.

During her nearly sixty-year professional career, Ella Fitzgerald earned fourteen Grammy Awards, the Presidential Medal of Freedom, and the respect of musicians and audiences throughout the world.

MILES DAVIS (1926–1991)

"Don't play what's there, play what's not there." —M. D.

A legendary trumpet player and jazz innovator, Miles Davis created cutting-edge music for over six decades despite battling a heroin addiction. His album *Kind of Blue* is one of the cornerstones of modern jazz with its cool, romantic, and melodic feel, lifting the constraints of structured chords[3] and granting the artist, as well as the audience, a newfound freedom.

Miles Davis. *Photofest © Photofest.*

"I'm always thinking about creating. My future starts when I wake up every morning. . . . Every day I find something creative to do with my life," said Davis. "For me, music and life are all about style."[4]

Raised during the Great Depression of the 1930s, Davis, who by his early teens had dedicated himself to the craft of music, eventually left East St. Louis for New York City and the Harlem jazz scene. There he attended the famed Julliard School, before dropping out to earn a living as a full-time musician. He began playing alongside his idol, saxophonist Charlie "Bird" Parker. Soon, they would play in each other's bands. Davis found himself in great demand. Over the coming decades, Miles Davis would change styles numerous times influencing many aspects of music, including the notion of "cool jazz." Besides his immense talent, Miles Davis constantly remained relevant and influential because he was always evolving as a musician.

"The thing to judge in any jazz artist is, does the man project and does he have ideas. When I'm playing, I'm never through. It's unfinished. I like to find a place to leave for someone else to finish it. That's where the high comes in," noted Davis of his lifelong pursuit of music.[5]

In 1989, along with author Quincy Troupe, Davis published his autobiography titled *Miles: The Autobiography*. He talks about his music, the periods of silence in his life (spurred by his drug use), and the racism he encountered, mostly in the United States, as a black musician.

Many of today's artists were in part inspired by the music of Miles Davis. Among them are Carlos Santana, John Mayer, DJ Premier, and John Legend.

"To our generation, Miles just represents cool. You look at the pictures and all the photography made him look like an icon who had his own unique thing and was so cool and comfortable in that thing," said John Legend. "He was a trendsetter. . . . I listened to *Kind Of Blue* all the time when I was in college, especially when I was studying. It's just so well put together—the music, the melodies, and the arrangements are all very subtle. I remember pretty much every moment and I can hum along to the whole record even now. It's all in my head, and any album I listened to that much has to make some impact on my own music."[6]

TIME TO DEBATE

Jazz soloists are known for their ability to improvise. However, you really don't want to create new reasoning on the fly during a debate or argument. How can you avoid this? Study your opponent's side of the argument. In fact, you should know it as well as your own. Anticipate what the opponent's main reasons will be to both support their point of view and attack yours. This should leave you on more than solid ground.

Is it possible the other side will come up with a reason or argument you hadn't envisioned? Yes, that can happen. And if it does, we hope you've learned something about improvisation from our pair of musical greats. Treat your argument like a song at a jazz concert. Let it always be the framework of what you present. If you need to improvise (or solo) a bit, always return to your planned speaking points and position before you conclude.

⑫

JOCKEY[1]

Angel Cordero Jr. vs. John Velazquez

Jockeys have an incredibly difficult and dangerous job. Usually weighing between 105 and 116 pounds, these unique individuals are perhaps the strongest pound-for-pound athletes in the world. The occupation demands it. Jockeys need to control and motivate 1,200-pound Thoroughbreds, often asking them to accelerate at nearly forty miles per hour through small openings in crowded fields of equine runners. Our debate for the G.O.A.T. in the jockey category is between two natives from the island of Puerto Rico—Angel Cordero Jr. and John Velazquez. To make our debate a little more interesting, Angel Cordero Jr. and John Velazquez are more than best friends. They have practically become family, ever since Cordero served as Velazquez's mentor many years ago.

ANGEL CORDERO JR. (B. 1942)

Growing up in Puerto Rico, Angel Cordero began grooming horses in the barn of his father, who was an ex-jockey. At sixteen, Cordero started sneaking back to the barn after school to ride. Sensing the competitive fire in his son, Cordero's father made a deal with him—finish high

Angel Cordero Jr.

school and I'll teach you to be a jockey. The teen practiced for hours a day, often using a hay bale as an imaginary horse. After years of hard work and dedication, Cordero became a champion jockey in Puerto Rico. Only he desperately wanted to prove himself in the United States and compete in the world's biggest races, such as the Kentucky Derby. During his first year in the States, Cordero was given few horses to ride. He became angry and frustrated over the lack of opportunity. So Angel packed his bags to fly home. That's when Eddie Belmonte, an older jockey who also hailed from Puerto Rico, wrestled the bags out of Cordero's hands. Belmonte gave his fellow countryman some tough love by calling him "chicken" and "quitter." That hurt Angel's pride, and he vowed to make his dream of riding in the United States a reality. Soon, an even more determined Cordero began to make his mark in the saddle, eventually winning three Kentucky Derbys. Trainers claimed that Angel was getting more out of their Thoroughbreds than any other jockey, that racehorses were responding to Angel's own tremendous energy and will to win.

JOHN VELAZQUEZ (B. 1971)

When John Velazquez was a youngster in Puerto Rico, his mother, understanding her son's desire to ride, bought him a broken-down horse for $100. That was a lot of money to the family, which eventually nursed the horse back to health so that John could ride it through the countryside. At the time, that John didn't even know that being a jockey was a job. That changed one day when a professional rider visited a family member living in his hometown. Suddenly, Velazquez's eyes were open to the possibility of a career riding Thoroughbreds. John went on to attend the famous Puerto Rico Jockey School and later began to win races on the island. Angel Cordero saw a tape of the young rider and contacted John, encouraging him to move to the United States.

Here's what happened almost two years later:

On January 12, 1992, a chilly wind blew through Aqueduct Racetrack in Queens, New York. Jockey Angel Cordero Jr. confidently strode into the paddock where eleven Thoroughbreds were being saddled to compete in the upcoming race. Cordero's confidence was

John Velazquez.

a reflection of his amazing ability as a rider—perhaps the greatest to ever live. It was a skill that won him more than seven thousand races. At forty-nine, Cordero, already a grandfather of two, was still competing when athletes his age in other sports had long since retired. The other jockeys, most of whom were young enough to be his grown sons, respected Cordero immensely for his intensely competitive nature. But they feared him too, knowing they could never rest for a second on the lead with Angel breathing down their necks.

Cordero approached his mount, Gray Tailwind, raising his left boot as the horse's trainer gave him a leg up into the saddle. Angel, by his own count, had been in twenty-three spills and broken nearly every bone in his body at least once. The flak jacket and helmet jockeys wear are a signal to how dangerous their profession can be. The ambulance that travels some one hundred yards behind the horses and riders as they race confirms it. But the fear of injury is something Cordero never let creep into his mind. For once a champion jockey's concern for his safety outweighs his desire to win, he is all but finished as a competitive rider.

On the racetrack, Cordero warmed up Grey Tailwind, just fifty yards or so from where twenty-year-old John Velazquez was warming up his horse, Deal Rowdy.

Velazquez had come to New York from his native Puerto Rico nearly two years before. He spoke little English at first and was invited to live with Cordero and his family until he could get settled. Angel then adopted John as his protégé and began teaching him everything he knew about riding racehorses. Why would Cordero share so much with Velazquez, with whom he would ride against every day in this highly competitive sport? Cordero was repaying the kindness another Puerto Rican rider, Eddie Belmonte, had shown him when he first came to this country and was struggling to find success.

The field of eleven Thoroughbreds approached the starting gate. Angel entered stall #2 on Grey Tailwind, and John #4 atop Deal Rowdy. Both riders sat ready to rush their horses from the starting gate in a three-quarter-mile sprint race. Then the sound of a bell split the air and the front doors of the starting gate sprung open. The ground shook with thundering hooves and dirt kicked up in every direction as the field furiously flew into stride.

Down along the inside rail, John pushed his horse to keep up behind the early leader. His hands and arms were pumping hard, but Deal Rowdy was already beginning to tire. Angel had Grey Tailwind racing along the inside rail too, behind John's horse. Only Cordero was sitting relaxed in the saddle, still waiting to make his move. As the field leaned into the far turn—leading to the stretch run and the finish line—Angel loosened his grip on the reins, giving Grey Tailwind his cue to accelerate. The Thoroughbred lengthened his stride and was gaining quickly. The rest was a blur to both Cordero and Velazquez.

Deal Rowdy's left leg suddenly snapped. John and his horse went crashing to the cold ground. It happened so fast, Cordero had nowhere to go. Grey Tailwind tripped over the fallen horse, and Angel was launched head over heels, somersaulting through the air. Angel slammed into one of the metal poles holding up the inside rail, and his battered body lay wrapped around it. Cordero and Velazquez were rushed to the hospital—both were unconscious.

John awoke in the same hospital room as Angel, his friend and mentor. At first, the young rider thought he was dreaming. Sadly, it was all too real. John was lucky. He had suffered only bumps and bruises. Angel, however, was hurt much worse. Cordero's right elbow and four of his ribs were broken. But the champion jockey had also suffered massive internal injuries. John felt terrible about the accident. There was no one to blame. The spill was a result of the risk riders take every time they go onto the racetrack.

That night, Angel told the doctors he could feel that he was bleeding internally. The doctors operated on Angel, removing his spleen, while John and Cordero's family prayed he'd survive.

Angel had nightmares for five straight nights, seeing himself somersaulting through the air. He spent nine days in intensive care and thirty-one days in the hospital overall before the doctors allowed him to go home. But the brave and resilient Cordero, whose passion for his sport was so strong, would eventually ride Thoroughbreds again.

Today, nearing the age of fifty, John Velazquez is one of the world's leading jockeys, having won over six thousand races and a trio of Kentucky Derbys, just like his mentor. He is the sport's all-time leading money winner, and Angel Cordero, now almost eighty, served as his agent for nearly three decades, booking him on mounts after his own riding career had ended. Both riders are masters of pace, seemingly with a stopwatch in their heads, rationing out a horse's speed over the course of a race. Both are also powerful finishers, motivating their mounts to stride forward toward the finish line. So who's the G.O.A.T. when it comes to being a jockey, Angel Cordero Jr. or John Velazquez? Is it the teacher or the student?

You can watch both Angel Cordero Jr. and John Velazquez ride their most masterful races on YouTube.

TIME TO DEBATE

Often in a debate, after you give a reason or "claim" supporting your position, someone on the other side of the argument will give a "counterclaim." A counterclaim aims to overcome your reasoning; to defeat it with a different and maybe more comprehensive view of the facts.

Debater #1 "Angel Cordero Jr. is the G.O.A.T. among jockeys. To prove it, he even taught someone else—John Velazquez—to be a great rider."

Debater #2: "Sure, at the start of his career, Velazquez was tutored by Cordero. But Velazquez always had his own greatness inside of him. You don't believe Cordero could have taught just anyone to be a top rider? Do you?"

13

MARTIAL ARTIST

Rickson Gracie vs. Bruce Lee

There are amazing martial artists who are accomplished fighters, and others who are talented teachers. The phrase "martial arts" means different things to different people. That's why it's a difficult task to try and isolate the G.O.A.T. in this category. There are more than a thousand martial arts systems and styles studied throughout the world, each usually boasting its own iconic practitioner. So please don't let this upcoming debate over the pair we've chosen devolve into an argument that goes beyond words, because martial arts are as much about peace as they are about conflict.

RICKSON GRACIE (B. 1958)

The Gracies are a legendary Brazilian Jiu-Jitsu family from Rio de Janeiro. Rickson Gracie is the son of Helio Gracie, who along with his brothers (Rickson's uncles) are considered the founding fathers of BJJ, a source of great sporting pride for the country of Brazil.[1] BJJ is a martial art with a strong focus on grappling and ground-fighting.

"Jiu-jitsu puts you completely in the moment, where you must have a complete focus on finding a solution to the problem. This trains the mind to build that focus, to increase your awareness, your capacity to solve problems," said Rickson Gracie.[2]

The Gracie family is recognized for taking part in many challenge matches against anyone willing to fight, no matter their style. Over time, this became the model on which today's professional mixed martial arts, or MMA, is based. Why is Rickson Gracie considered among the greatest martial artists of all time? Well, he is undefeated in eleven professional MMA matches against a wide variety of the world's top practitioners. Rickson defeated fighters of varying styles, including a Japanese Jiu-Jitsu champion, a kickboxing champion, and a Japanese wrestling champion. Rickson Gracie is recognized as a master of submission—forcing an opponent to quit or tap-out. In one form or another, Rickson "submitted" all eleven of his professional opponents. He is considered a true pioneer in bringing both BJJ and MMA to people around the world.[3]

Rickson is recognized for his relentless work ethic, constantly refining his grappling techniques and trying to improve himself as a martial artist. Rickson also possesses unbelievable mental fortitude and concentration, always believing that he is the best competitor.

"The journey has to be based on passion. Put yourself in something you love to do. If you love what you do you're able to dedicate yourself, overcome obstacles," noted Gracie.

He is the subject of a 1995 documentary titled *Choke*, which is one of the methods for submitting an opponent in BJJ. In the 2008 film *The Incredible Hulk*, Rickson plays a martial arts instructor helping Dr. Bruce Banner—Hulk's alter ego—to gain balance in his life.

"The biggest gift I received as a martial artist is without a question the capacity to be in peace," said Rickson Gracie of his personal journey.[4]

BRUCE LEE (1940–1973)

Bruce Lee, as the world came to know him, was born Lee Jun-fan in San Francisco, California. He lived to be just thirty-two years old. It was a comparatively short life span considering the monumental impact Bruce Lee made on martial arts and the entertainment industry. Lee spent his adolescence in Hong Kong, where his father was a well-known member of the Chinese opera—the equivalent of a

Bruce Lee. *Twentieth Century Fox Film Corp./ Photofest © Twentieth Century Fox Film Corp.*

top-charting pop star in today's society. That connection to the world of performance gave a young Bruce Lee the opportunity to be cast in several films as a child actor, honing his dynamic on-screen personality. As Lee entered his teens, with Hong Kong being home to a multitude of street gangs and organized crime families called *triads*, fighting and martial arts became part of his everyday existence. Bruce Lee was involved in countless fights to defend himself, including at school. His parents were warned their son would be arrested if this behavior continued. Eventually, Lee's family sent Bruce to live in the United States with his sister. He enrolled in the University of Washington, studying philosophy and psychology.

Lee began to teach martial arts in the United States. He taught anyone who he believed had a pure heart, regardless of the student's ethnicity or skin color. Some of the older masters in San Francisco's Chinatown didn't like that. They believed that martial arts were for those of pure Asian blood only. Lee had experienced the same type of prejudice himself while studying in Hong Kong, because his mother was part European. Those masters sent their champion to fight Lee at his school. If Lee won, he could continue to teach anyone he wanted. But if Lee lost, he'd have to conform to their rules. Bruce won that fight, but he was unhappy at the amount of time it took him to defeat their champion, so he began to train even harder.

"I'm not in this world to live up to your expectations and you're not in this world to live up to mine," said Lee.[5]

Lee was a voracious reader and liked to carry a book with him wherever he went. He had a personal library containing over 2,500 books. They were not limited to books on martial arts and other forms of combat. Eastern and Western philosophy were also of great interest to him.

As a martial artist, Lee, who stood 5 foot 7 and weighed approximately 140 pounds, was recognized for his combination of raw power and blinding speed. To fit his particular strengths, Lee invented his own martial art called *Jeet Kune Do*, which translates from Cantonese as "the way of the intercepting fist." The hybrid art blends together aspects of Kung Fu, western boxing, fencing, and several other forms of self-defense. Lee did not want to be restricted by any one rigid style.

"Empty your mind, be formless. Shapeless, like water. If you put water into a cup, it becomes the cup. You put water into a bottle and it becomes the bottle. You put it in a teapot, it becomes the teapot. Now, water can flow or it can crash. Be water, my friend," noted Lee.[6]

Because of his success in combining different martial arts, Bruce Lee is widely considered to be the forerunner of today's mixed martial arts (MMA) competitors.

Lee starred in several classic martial arts films, including *Way of the Dragon* (1972), which contains an iconic fight scene inside the Roman Coliseum against karate champion Chuck Norris. Through his films, Bruce Lee is often credited with changing the way Asians were perceived in American culture, shifting them away from stereotypical roles as servants or restaurant workers.

In July 1973, Bruce Lee died of a cerebral edema, after complaining of headaches.

TIME TO DEBATE

It's too bad that Bruce Lee and Rickson Gracie never competed against one another. That would have given us a more conclusive answer in our martial arts G.O.A.T. debate. But there is one thing we can be certain about—each would have truly respected the other.

Pro fighters make a habit of mixing it up. Of course, they are supposed to adhere to the rules of the contest, usually with a referee in attendance. Formal debates have moderators in charge. They act as the refs, enforcing the rules and protocols. Whether you're in a formal debate or a friendly argument, remember your remarks should never get too personal concerning your opponent. That's not good debate, and could easily lead to a total breakdown in communication. Notice what happens with our debaters below. Do either of them truly "win" the debate with remarks like these?

Debater #1: "I should have expected an opinion like that from you. I can't remember when you've ever seen things clearly."

Debater #2: "That's so insulting. I'm not even going to speak to you now."

LIGHTNING DEBATE

Imagine that you could have Bruce Lee as your personal bodyguard for one day. Your school's biggest bully walks down the hallway straight toward you, with a look on his face as though he'll be asking for trouble. Now, would you give that bully a warning about Bruce or leave him to learn his own lesson?

WHAT IS KUNG FU?

There are over five hundred different styles or systems of Kung Fu, each one unique and often very different from the others. They all have something in common, however, that makes them part of the Kung Fu family. What's that? The answer can be found in the literal meaning of Kung Fu, which translates from Cantonese as "time and effort equals a skill." Fighting isn't the only thing to which the term Kung Fu applies. For example, stores can be called Kung Fu Bakery or Kung Fu Tea, meaning the people who work there have spent lots of time and effort to learn how to bake excellent bread or brew outstanding tea. Also, a person who is friendly and honorable, qualities more revered in Asian culture than the ability to fight, are said to have "good Kung Fu."

14

MATHEMATICAN

Srinivasa Ramanujan vs. Sir Isaac Newton

Go to your math teacher today and ask for their thoughts on who is the greatest mathematician of all time. After reading about our two entries for the G.O.A.T. in this category, you'll probably have your own opinion to share. After all, we're all about proving to your teachers how smart you are. We're also not above trying to snag you some extra credit for presenting a solid argument.

SRINIVASA RAMANUJAN (1887–1920)

Here's a name you may have never encountered before: Srinivasa Ramanujan, who was born in India and grew up in extreme poverty. From an early age, Ramanujan was obsessed with mathematics. He didn't have much formal training in the subject, though. Instead, he was self-taught, learning from math books. Early on in his math career, people were doubtful of his amazing results because he'd never learned to show all of his work, proving how he'd come to his conclusions. (I suppose you've heard that particular complaint before from your own math teachers.) Ramanujan become so intensely focused on math that the rest of his studies suffered terribly. He eventually gained a math scholarship to college, but he did so poorly in his other

Srinivasa Ramanujan.

subjects that it was taken away. Undeterred, he continued to study math on his own. Then, with the help and guidance of other mathematicians who recognized his genius, Ramanujan moved from India to England where he earned a degree at Cambridge University.[1]

Among Ramanujan's mathematical triumphs is recognizing an infinite series for π (Pi or 3.14), which calculates the number based on the summation of other numbers. This infinite series serves as the basis for many algorithms used to calculate π. There are several outstanding books written about Ramanujan, including *The Man Who Knew Infinity* by Robert Kanigel, which was made into a 2015 film of the same title.

How much did mathematics mean to Srinivasa Ramanujan? While he was sick in a hospital bed, not long before his death at the mere age of thirty-two, a friend and fellow mathematician came to visit him. The visitor remarked that he'd arrived in cab number 1729. Ramanujan almost instantly recognized it as a special number—the smallest number expressible as the sum of two cubes in two different ways.

The two different ways are: $1729 = 1^3 + 12^3 = 9^3 + 10^3$. It has since become known in math circles as the "Taxicab Number."[2]

SIR ISAAC NEWTON (1643–1727)

You probably know the English mathematician, physicist, and astronomer Sir Isaac Newton from the story of him sitting beneath an apple tree. The legend goes that he was hit on the head with a piece of falling fruit, inspiring an "aha moment" and thus causing him to formulate the law of universal gravitation—things always fall downward, not up or sideways. There's no evidence that the apple actually hit Newton, who was at his parents farm due to Cambridge University closing because of the Bubonic Plague (a deadly pandemic of the seventeenth century).[3] The falling fruit, however, did make a significant mental impression on him.

As a mathematician, Newton saw a relationship between physical events and the mathematics of the day, bringing about a whole new math inspired by his conceptual understanding of physics.[4] His theory of calculus—that's right, if you have trouble with that subject in school, blame Newton—allowed mathematicians to make sense of motion and dynamic change in the world around us. Those dynamic changes included the orbits of planets and the motion of fluids. He also developed a formula to approximate the slope of a curve, still used today in everything from plotting the path of a satellite circling the earth to measuring the break on a curveball released from the hand of a pitcher in baseball.[5]

After learning about both of our entries, who's your choice for the G.O.A.T. in the field of mathematics? Maybe your math teacher will have a personal favorite we didn't include. There are plenty of other worthy people to consider. For example, Archimedes was an ancient Greek who recognized the principle of buoyancy (why things float) and the mathematical principles of how a lever allows you to hoist great weight. There's also Carl Friedrich Gauss, a German mathematician, who contributed greatly to number theory, algebra, astronomy, analysis, and differential geometry. You know he had to be smart.

TIME TO DEBATE

Who decides the winner to a debate or argument? Less formal arguments are mostly decided by the participants. Often, each side believes that it got the better of the other. If you're truthful with yourself, though, you probably have an accurate idea of how you actually did. Are there things that you wish you had said better or differently? Were there important points that you forgot to make? That's always a good indicator that you might have performed better. Don't stress it. That's what practice is for.

Formal debates, however, are scored by a judge who usually uses a "rubric" or scoring guide. A debate rubric mostly looks at categories such as clarity and organization of your argument, your claims, counterclaims and refutations, as well as your presentation style.

Who's the G.O.A.T. among mathematicians? Make your arguments and let the judges give their scores. Ah, using math to settle a debate about mathematicians. That *figures* perfectly.

Maybe you like math-themed books and movies. If so, read *Hidden Figures: The American Dream and Untold Story of the Black Women Mathematicians Who Helped Win the Space Race* by Margot Lee Shetterly. The book details the hard work and social obstacles encountered by Dorothy Vaughan, Mary Jackson, Katherine Johnson, and Christine Darden, four African American women who endured Virginia's Jim Crow laws while working at NASA's Langley Air Force Base in the 1960s. The women, known as "human computers," used pencils, slide rules, and adding machines to calculate the correct paths for our rockets and astronauts to successfully fly missions and safely return to earth. In 2016, *Hidden Figures* became a movie and was nominated for three Academy Awards. Likewise, *A Beautiful Mind* by Sylvia Nash is the powerful biography of math genius John Nash, who overcame serious mental challenges to win the Nobel Prize. Actor Russell Crowe starred in the 2001 film version of the book, which received the Academy Award for Best Picture.

(15)

MC (HIP-HOP ARTIST)

Nas vs. Jay-Z

The roots of hip-hop began in the Bronx, New York, aka The Boogie Down Bronx, in the late 1970s. A song by the Sugarhill Gang titled "Rapper's Delight" featured the lyrics, "I said a hip, hop, the hippie the hippie to the hip hip hop, and you don't stop." With that phrase the beginning of a culture was born. An MC or "Master of Ceremonies" would take the center stage—even if that stage was a street corner or living room at a house party—and lay down their best rhymes. Hip-hop is organic. Music companies don't anoint MCs. The listeners do. They're the ones who give the ultimate stamp of approval, making stars out of street poets. Who's the greatest MC of all time? The potential list is long, filled with talented artists, each with a slightly different slant on the genre. Nevertheless, we've chosen a pair to do battle at the mic, as it should be for dueling MCs. They can both figuratively spit fire so make sure to keep out of the way.

NAS (B. 1973)

> "Hip-hop is the streets . . . that feel of music with urgency that speaks to you. It speaks to your livelihood and it's not compromised. It's blunt. It's raw, straight off the street—from the beat to the voice to the words." —N. B. O. D. J.

A product of New York's City's Queensbridge Houses, Nasir Bin Olu Dara Jones, who is better known to music fans as Nas, is perhaps hip-hop's greatest storyteller. His protagonists and antagonists, heroes and antiheroes, inhabit a stark inner-city landscape that is never devoid of hope.

"I can be. B-boys and girls, listen up. . . . If the truth is told, the youth can grow. Then learn to survive until they gain control. Nobody says you have to be gangstas, hoes. Read more, learn more. Change the globe. Ghetto children, do your thing. Hold your head up, little man, you're a king."

"Young princess, when you get your wedding ring. Your man is saying, 'She's my queen.'"

It should be no surprise that Nas was born to flow. His father was a jazz musician named Olu Dara, who studied piano and clarinet. As

NAS. *Photofest © Photofest.*

a youngster, Nas or Nasir, which means helper or protector in Arabic, played his father's trumpet.[1] In fact, the MC has been instrumental in trying to keep alive after-school music programs. Nas himself dropped out after the eighth grade. So he understands how difficult it can be for adolescents with a passion for music to maintain a connection to their school.

"I want to sound like an instrument. I want my voice and my words to marry the beat," said Nas. "I go with the rhythm of it and the words start to come to my mind and those words could be based on things that (have) been on my mind for the past year, the past month, the past week, whatever; I write it."[2]

Nas's 1994 debut album *Illmatic* is hailed by fans, his hip-hop peers, and music critics alike, as one of the most honest and illuminating representations of inner-city life ever recorded. It is often referred to as the "Hip-hop Bible." Filmmakers Erik Parker and Anthony Saleh were so moved by the totality of the work that they made a 2004 documentary about it titled *Time Is Illmatic*, highlighted by revealing interviews with Nas and his father.

In a 2012 interview, Nas explained his motivation. "My rap generation started, it was about bringing you inside my apartment. It wasn't about being a rap star; it was about anything other than. I want you to know who I am: what the streets taste like, feel like, smell like. . . . It was important to me that I told the story that way because I thought that it wouldn't be told if I didn't tell it. . . . That needed to be documented and my life needed to be told."[3]

JAY-Z (B. 1969)

> "Shakespeare was a man who wrote poetry. I'm a man who writes poetry. Why not compare yourself to the best?" —S. C.

Another artist inspired by the streets of New York City, Shawn Carter is better known throughout the hip-hop and business world as Jay-Z. But let's leave Jay-Z's ultrasuccessful business ventures such as Roc-A-Fella Records, Rocawear (clothing), and Roc Nation (management) aside and concentrate solely on the music.

Jay-Z's smooth voice can blend effortlessly into any rhythm, tempo, or emotion a song might need to evoke. It has the sharpness to cut through the bass line while still being relaxed enough to massage a rhyme or off-rhyme at a line's end.

Growing up in Brooklyn's Marcy Projects, Jay-Z's environment presented him with story after story—places to be, places not to be—all filled to the brim with the soul and fortitude of the people living their lives around him. And though he'd become bored with high school, there was a spark inside of him to write that wouldn't cool.

Jay-Z. *Photofest © Photofest.*

"I would run into the corner store, the bodega, and just grab a paper bag or buy juice, anything just to get a paper bag. And I'd write the words on the paper bag and stuff these ideas in my pocket until I got back. Then I would transfer them into the notebook," said Jay-Z.[4]

At the beginning of his journey, Jay-Z couldn't get a record deal. Instead, he sold CDs out of the trunk of his car, proving there was an appetite on the street for what he had to communicate. Along with a pair of other artists, Jay-Z cofounded Roc-A-Fella Records, which became the outlet for his first album, *Reasonable Doubt* (1996).

Empowerment has always been at the core of Jay-Z's lyrics. They're mostly about self-worth and independence, urging people to lift themselves up and to strive for something better.[5] And the image of the artist—sometimes inhabiting the background, other times being front and center—is always there to deliver the message.

"*I'm forever young. My name shall survive, Through the darkest blocks, over kitchen stoves, over Pyrex pots, my name shall be passed down to generations while debating up in barber shops. Young slung, hung here. . . . With a little ambition just what we can become here . . . as the father passed his story down to his son's ears.*"

Though he can superbly relate a lyric written about a small, personal moment, Jay-Z's eyes also focus on the bigger picture. That includes hip-hop's stake in a larger society, as a reflection of inner-city streets and the invisible borders that often separate us.

"Hip-hop has done so much for racial relations, and I don't think it's given the proper credit," said Jay-Z. "It has changed America immensely. I'm going to make a very bold statement: Hip-hop has done more than any leader, politician, or anyone to improve race relations."[6]

A member of the Songwriters Hall of Fame, Jay-Z has sold over fifty million albums and been honored with more than twenty Grammy Awards.

TIME TO DEBATE

When selecting the G.O.A.T. among hip-hop artists, you might want to consider their ability to flow, to deliver their rhymes smoothly and effortlessly. It's the same for debaters. Having a smooth delivery and gliding from one segment of your argument to the next can influence the listener. To that end, using segues or transitional phrases—language that can seamlessly connect one idea to another—will help achieve that goal. Some examples of these are: to begin with, for instance, despite, therefore, on the contrary, for this reason, as you can see, however, therefore, and as you can see.

Debater #1: "Nas was never looking to become a rap star. However, his natural talent basically propelled him to the top of the hip-hop world on its own."

Debater#2: "To begin with, the incredible combination of Jay-Z's smooth voice and empowering lyrics clearly make him the greatest MC of all time."

By the way (another transition phrase), judges in debates also flow. How so? The note-taking process they use while debaters are arguing their points is actually called "flowing."

WOMEN ON THE MIC

The latter-half of the 1980s saw the rise of women MCs such as New Jersey's Queen Latifa (Dana Owens) and Brooklyn's MC Lyte (Lana Michele Moorer). Both artists were hugely successful and their work critically acclaimed for presenting a feminist viewpoint. Recently, though, there has been a notable absence of female voices in hip-hop. Queen Latifa is even making a documentary film about the current dearth of women on the mic.

MC Lyte believes it may be caused by the misogynistic treatment of women in some hip-hop lyrics. "[That disrespect has] literally broken down our character," she noted. "It has gotten to the point that we have been subjected to such harsh verbal treatment, assassinated even, that who would want to listen [to women MCs]?"[7]

Queen Latifa draws the line at lyrics portraying women in a negative light. "I always wanted my mother to be able to play my records. I would much rather have my mother's respect than just have a bunch of money and buy her houses, but not have her respect. (I wanted) for someone to be able to mention my name and her say, 'Oh, that's my daughter!' and feel proud of that."[8]

16

ORATOR (PUBLIC SPEAKER)

Martin Luther King Jr. vs. Sir Winston Churchill

Throughout history, there have been many marvelous orators, a fancy word for public speakers. They include powerful wordsmiths such as Nelson Mandela, Gandhi, John F. Kennedy, Ruth Bader Ginsburg, Abraham Lincoln, Frederick Douglass, and Sojourner Truth. In the cases of Lincoln, Douglass, and Truth, we do not even have historical recordings of their voices. To be recognized this long with this type of regard, you know that their words must be extremely powerful. But who is the oratory G.O.A.T.? We have assembled a pair of incredible candidates for you to choose from below.

MARTIN LUTHER KING JR. (1929–1968)

Born in Atlanta, Georgia, Marin Luther King Jr. was a preacher and civil rights advocate who focused on nonviolent resolutions to the problem of systemic racism. He is simply hailed as one of the greatest orators to ever stand at a podium and address a crowd. His most famous speech, titled *I Have a Dream*, was delivered at the March on Washington for Jobs and Freedom on August 28, 1963, in front of the Lincoln Memorial. King's words and the passion of his presentation, touching both a raw nerve and hope in American society, have made this seventeen-minute long speech one of the most iconic moments in our nation's history. Speaking in the shadow of Abraham Lincoln, King begins his speech with the phrase, "Five score years ago." It is a nod to the renowned speaking prowess of Lincoln who began his famed Gettysburg Address with, "Four score and seven years ago." A score is equal to twenty years, and Lincoln was referring back to the date when the Declaration of Independence was signed. King's "five score" is meant to recall the date, 1863, in which Lincoln signed the Emancipation Proclamation, theoretically freeing all slaves.

"This momentous decree came as a great beacon light of hope to millions of Negro slaves who had been seared in the flames of withering injustice. It came as a joyous daybreak to end the long night of their captivity . . . [but] it is obvious today that America has defaulted on this promissory note insofar as her citizens of color are concerned. Instead of honoring this sacred obligation, America has given the Negro people a bad check, a check that has come back marked 'insufficient funds,'" spoke King, comparing America's failure to provide equal rights to people of color with the government defaulting on an invaluable payment owed them.

After stirring people's emotions, King is careful to remind the protestors not to sink to the depths of their oppressors by answering violence with a violent reaction of their own.

"But there is something that I must say to my people who stand on the warm threshold which leads into the palace of justice. In the process of gaining our rightful place we must not be guilty of wrongful deeds. Let us not seek to satisfy our thirst for freedom by drinking from the cup of bitterness and hatred. We must forever conduct our struggle on the high plane of dignity and discipline. We must not allow our creative protest to degenerate into physical violence. Again and again we must rise to the majestic heights of meeting physical force with soul force."

(*Note the alliteration in the string of Ds provided by "dignity," "discipline," and "degenerate.")*

King then emphasizes the image of the "dream," something that is not currently a reality, but offering hope that it is still within our grasp.

The speaker then combines that with a sound image of the Liberty Bell, which in reality contains a sizable crack.

(Notice the upcoming repetition of "I have a dream," "one day," and "nation." This tool used to grab the listener's attention is called "anaphora." It's defined as the repetition of phrases, words, clauses, sentences, or lines.)

"I have a dream that one day this nation will rise up and live out the true meaning of its creed: We hold these truths to be self-evident, that all men are created equal. . . . I have a dream that my four little children will one day live in a nation where they will not be judged by the color of their skin but by the content of their character. . . . And if America is to be a great nation, this must become true. And so let freedom ring from the prodigious hilltops of New Hampshire. Let freedom ring from the mighty mountains of New York. Let freedom ring from the heightening Alleghenies of Pennsylvania. . . . But not only that; let freedom ring from Stone Mountain of Georgia. . . ."

Tragically, King's second iconic speech, *I've Been to the Mountaintop*, delivered in Memphis, Tennessee, on April 3, 1968, foreshadowed his assassination less than twenty-four hours later. He was speaking in Memphis because the city's sanitation workers, who were mostly Black, were striking.

"But it really doesn't matter with me now, because I've been to the mountaintop . . . I've seen the Promised Land. I may not get there with you. But I want you to know tonight, that we, as a people, will get to the Promised Land," said King in a testament to his faith.

You can hear both the *I Have a Dream* and *I've Been to the Mountaintop* speeches in their entirety on YouTube.

SIR WINSTON CHURCHILL (1874–1965)

> *"You have enemies? Good. That means you've stood up for something, sometime in your life."* —W. C.

Could a person's ability to speak and motivate others with his confident tone and passionate words have really changed the outcome of World War II? Many historians believe that Sir Winston Churchill, who served his first term as prime minister of England from 1940 to 1945, during the height of that war, did just that. The terrible conflict was not going well for the British. The island nation was being bombed unmercifully by Adolph Hitler and his Nazi regime. Germany's full-out continuous attacks on many different battle fronts at once were referred to as the "blitz" or "blitzkrieg." These devastating raids were making a huge impact. France, an ally of England, along with the United States and Russia, had already fallen to Germany and was being occupied by Nazi troops. England was concerned that it could suffer the same fate, losing its independence. That's where Churchill's great ability as an orator proved invaluable. He delivered a number of speeches to his country, mostly over the BBC (British Broadcasting Corporation) radio network, inspiring Englanders to find the strength to fight back during the darkest of times.

Concerning the gift of speech, Churchill noted, "Of all the talents bestowed upon men, none is so precious as the gift of oratory. He who enjoys it wields a power more durable than that of a great king. He is an independent force in the world. Abandoned by his party, betrayed by his friends, stripped of his offices, whoever can command this power is still formidable."

Of course, it wasn't just Churchill's words that inspired his people. His physical image played an important role as well. The prime minister was often photographed touring the damage of sites that had been bombed. He walked through such devastated scenes with complete confidence, smoking a cigar and flashing a V-sign for victory.[1]

"We shall defend our island, whatever the cost may be, we shall fight on the beaches, we shall fight on the landing grounds, we shall fight in the fields and in the streets, we shall fight in the hills; we shall never surrender," emphasized Churchill, igniting Englanders in a common goal.

Here is a portion of Churchill's *This Was Their Finest Hour* speech delivered in the British House of Commons on June 18, 1940. The passion behind these words is credited with helping a nation to face its enemies under the direst of circumstances:

Upon this battle depends the survival of Christian civilization. Upon it depends our own British life, and the long continuity of our institutions and our Empire. The whole fury and might of the enemy must very soon be turned upon us. Hitler knows that he will have to break us in this island or lose the war. If we can stand up to him, all Europe may be free and the life of the world may move forward into broad, sunlit uplands. But if we fail, then the whole world, including the United States, including all that we have known and cared for, will sink into the abyss of a new Dark Age. . . . Let us therefore brace ourselves to our duties, and so bear ourselves that, if the British Empire and its Commonwealth last for a thousand years, men will still say, "This was their finest hour."[2]

YouTube boasts a full complement of Churchill's most inspiring speeches. Give them a listen and see if you agree with the historians about how important they were in bolstering his people's fighting spirit.

TIME TO DEBATE

Do you like to speak in public? Who's the best speaker in your class? Does your school have a debate team? If you're interested in starting one, you might want to talk to a teacher about being the team's coach or advisor. Hey, that could be a real test of your ability as an orator— to convince a teacher to take on that role! And if you really practice and work diligently at it, maybe one day people will mention your name whenever they discuss the greatest orators of all time.

There's little doubt that most of the great orators were born with a natural ability to communicate. But that natural ability also needs to be nurtured. That usually happens through practice. How can you find a potential audience whenever you need one? Simply practice by speaking in front of a mirror. It will give you the opportunity to view yourself as a speaker and begin to refine any negatives of which you become aware.

LIGHTNING DEBATE

You want to go with your friends to a certain event. Your parents are hesitant to allow you to attend. You feel that you haven't presented a strong enough case in your own favor. If you could call on an orator, either an historical or current-day speaker to approach your parents on your behalf, who would it be and why?

17

PHILOSOPHER

Plato vs. Albert Camus

Do you have a personal philosophy, a system of beliefs by which your life is guided? Is it simply to get to the cafeteria on Taco Tuesday before there is nothing left but cracked shells and shredded cheese? Well, if your own philosophy—even if you're still refining one for yourself—runs somewhat deeper than that, you'll enjoy our debate on who is the greatest philosopher of all time.

PLATO (429–347 B.C.E.)

"I'm trying to think. Don't confuse me with the facts." —P.

Plato was a Greek philosopher and author who tackled the major events of his time, including politics and intellectual movements. But it is his rich and suggestive philosophy that has excited readers for more than two centuries, causing many succeeding philosophers to be profoundly influenced by him. Being influenced in your thinking by Plato makes you a Platonist. Almost all of Plato's writings come in the form of dialogues between characters (mostly real people)—which establish an initial setting such as a prison, gymnasium, celebration, a stroll outside of the city's walls, or a walk on a rain-soaked day. Plato pondered the ideas or forms of religion, science, human nature, love, and sexuality.

He denied the reality of the material world, considering it to only be a copy of the real world. Plato believed that at a minimum there were two worlds: a world of concrete objects which constantly changed before our senses and an unchanging, unseen world of ideas and abstract objects grasped only by pure reason. Things like boulders, columns, buildings, and chairs belonged to the material world, while concepts such as justice, truth, and beauty can only truly inhabit the unseen world.[1]

"We can easily forgive a child who is afraid of the dark," wrote Plato. "The real tragedy of life is when men are afraid of the light."[2] Plato described this difference as "Being" and "Becoming." The world of *Being* rests outside of time and space, where everything is perfect. However, we mostly make our way through the imperfect world of *Becoming*, enduring the struggle in hopes of reaching that perfect plane.

How has Plato influenced our world today? Plato thought it was very important to educate would-be statesmen or politicians. So he established a school for future leaders. That school was called the Academy, named for the park in which it was situated. That's the origin of the word "academic," meaning *having to do with education*.

The philosopher conceived of the mythical underwater city of Atlantis. It was mentioned as part of a parable (a story used to teach a lesson) in his final dialogue *Timaeus*, and also in *Critias*. The term Platonic love (a close relationship without sex between two people) is also inspired by Plato, though the philosopher never used the term himself. Also, almost all that we know of the great philosopher Socrates, who was Plato's teacher, comes from Plato's dialogues.[3]

ALBERT CAMUS (1913–1960)

Much of Albert Camus's (pronounced Ka-moo) philosophy can be seen in his work as a journalist, playwright, novelist, and author of short stories. He even denied being a philosopher. Yet despite that claim, he is recognized as one of the most important and influential philosophers ever. A French-Algerian, Camus, who was born in North Africa, is widely known for his thoughts on the absurdity of life—focusing on the onslaught of obstacles that often make negotiating the world an incredibly difficult uphill task. To illustrate this, he wrote *The Myth of Sisyphus*, building on the ancient myth of King Sisyphus, who in being punished by the gods was forced to continually push a giant boulder to the top of a steep hill, only to have it roll back down again before reaching the summit.

"Sometimes, carrying on, just carrying on, is the superhuman achievement," said Camus.

Perhaps Camus's thoughts on life can best be understood knowing that both World War I and World War II raged during his forty-seven-year life span. He even joined the resistance movement known as "the underground" when Nazi Germany invaded and occupied France,[4] fighting against Hitler's forces. Instead of toting a gun, he became editor of an outlawed newspaper called *Combat*. Despite witnessing those bloody wars and mass killings, Camus believed that people shouldn't waste or surrender their time on Earth, no matter how absurdly the universe might treat them.

"In the midst of hate, I found there was, within me, an invincible love. In the midst of tears, I found there was, within me, an invincible smile. In the midst of chaos, I found there was, within me, an invincible calm. . . . In the midst of winter, I found there was, within me, an invincible summer. And that makes me happy. For it says that no matter how hard the world pushes against me, within me, there's something stronger—something better, pushing right back," said Camus, who was awarded the 1957 Nobel Prize for Literature for a body of work that included his novels *The Stranger*, *The Plague*, and *The Fall*.[5]

TIME TO DEBATE

High schools and middle schools usually don't offer a class in philosophy. But you might want to debate the G.O.A.T. among philosophers with your history or English teacher. Philosophers are often quoted, giving us their exact words and thoughts on a particular subject. Debaters often use well-known quotes in their arguments to support their position. Here's how it's done.

Debater #1: "When Plato said, 'The real tragedy is when men are afraid of the light,' he meant that we shouldn't close our eyes to the truth out of fear."

Debater #2: "My philosophy has been to never give in to difficult circumstances. Like Albert Camus says, 'No matter how hard the world pushes against me, within me, there's something stronger— something better, pushing right back.' That's how I want to be."

Besides our entries in this category—Plato and Albert Camus— there have been many other noteworthy voices discussing the condition of humanity and our relationship to the universe. Most recognized among those voices are philosophers such as Lao-Tzu (sixth to fourth century BCE), Confucius (551–479 BCE), Immanuel Kant (1724–1804), and Karl Marx (1818–1883). Read their works and ideas. Maybe one of them will strike a chord with you or help you to define your own philosophy.

18

QUARTERBACK

Joe Montana vs. Tom Brady

Perhaps the position of quarterback is the most valuable in all of sports. Almost every football play begins with the quarterback touching the ball—whether he passes, hands off, or scrambles with the ball himself. For that reason, modern NFL franchises have their biggest investments, in the form of resources and salary, invested in their signal callers. Who's the G.O.A.T. among QBs? Names like Joe Namath, Johnny Unitas, Dan Marino, and "Slingin'" Sammy Baugh, who refined the art of the forward pass, all come to mind. During the past two decades, however, the pair of quarterbacks discussed below has dominated the debate.

JOE MONTANA (B. 1956)

When your nickname is "Joe Cool" and you're playing a high-pressure position such as NFL quarterback, you're obviously doing something at an apex level. As a senior in college, Pennsylvania native Joe Montana led the Notre Dame Fighting Irish to the 1977 National Championship in football. "Winners, I am convinced, imagine their dreams first. They want it with all their heart and expect it to come true. There is, I believe, no other way to live," said Montana.[1]

A steal in the third-round of the NFL draft (the eighty-second player selected), Montana was chosen by the San Francisco 49ers, a team named after the California Gold Rush of 1849. Appropriately, Montana brought the franchise and his teammates plenty of gold in the form of four championship rings. A perfect four-for-four in Super Bowls, the superbly talented signal caller was the game's MVP in three of them. Recognized for his incredible passing touch, feathering the football into extremely small windows, Montana was also light on his feet. Whenever he escaped the passing pocket and was called on to improvise a play, his outstanding football IQ mostly led to big trouble for opposing defenses.

Of course, Montana was fortunate enough to throw passes to arguably the greatest receiver to ever play football—Jerry Rice. But stuck behind Montana on the bench for several years was future Hall of Fame QB Steve Young. How good do you have to be to keep Steve Young on the bench? Good doesn't cut it. You have to be great.

"My mother and father—Joe and Theresa Montana—brought me along and taught me to never quit, and to strive to be the best," said the legendary quarterback.

Twice the NFL's MVP, an entire era of young quarterbacks grew up wishing they could be like their hero Joe Montana. What's it like to be the focal point of such admiration?

"Yeah, it's nice to look up to people, but the more you try to be somebody else, the less you are of yourself," noted Montana.[2]

Joe Montana met his future wife, Jennifer, while shooting a shaving commercial for TV. Now that's a "Joe Cool" move.

TOM BRADY (B. 1977)

Just like Joe Montana, Tom Brady's talent eluded the eyes of pro scouts. Only Brady was an even bigger steal in the NFL draft as the 199th selection in 2000 as he exited the University of Michigan.

Brady went to the New England Patriots with few expectations, except as possibly becoming a backup quarterback. As a rookie,

Brady even felt the need to introduce himself to the team's owner, Robert Kraft, just to make certain the boss knew his name. Soon the entire sports world would recognize Tom Brady as an unparalleled winner.

"Tom Terrific" delivered New England six Super Bowl titles in nine trips to the championship game. Brady is an admitted workaholic, practicing tirelessly and asking the same of his teammates. Over the seasons, the quarterback has even had several teammates live at his house, especially his receivers, so that he could develop a better rapport with them. But when this signal caller doesn't believe that others around him are giving their best, he's been known to openly admonish unfocused players, both on the sideline and on the field.

"A lot of times I find that people who are blessed with the most talent don't ever develop that attitude, and the ones who aren't blessed in that way are the most competitive and have the biggest heart," said Brady, who has garnered four Super Bowl MVPs while with the Pats. "To me, football is so much about mental toughness, it's digging deep, it's doing whatever you need to do to help a team win and that comes in a lot of shapes and forms."[3]

The quarterback, a California native, doesn't possess superior footspeed or the strongest arm. But Brady's ability to see and dissect the field in front of him and process information in real-time has set him far apart from his rivals.

Playing and producing at a high level well into his forties, Brady is a fitness and nutrition fanatic, taking incredible care of his body in an effort to prolong his career.

"I just love working hard. I love being part of a team. I love working toward a common goal."[4]

In 2020, Tom Brady ended his long relationship with the New England Patriots and began a new chapter in his career by signing with the Tampa Bay Buccaneers. In his first season with the Florida-based team, he led the Bucs to a Super Bowl victory, turning Tampa Bay into *Champ-a-Bay*. That marked Brady's tenth Super Bowl appearance and seventh victory, both records. He also collected his fifth Super Bowl MVP in that game.

One day in the future, this multiple-time NFL MVP will certainly waltz into the Hall of Fame on the first ballot.

TIME TO DEBATE

Quarterbacks at every level—from high school to the pros—put in an immense amount of study time, learning both their own playbook and opposing defenses. It's the same way for debaters, who often do a lot of research in preparing for a debate topic. That research could come in the form of speaking with people to hear their opinions, as well as gathering stats and information from appropriate sources like the library or internet. It's always good, though, to carefully scrutinize your potential sources to make sure they're not biased or slanted excessively pro (for) or con (against) on either side of the argument. That's why it's always a good idea to have multiple sources from which to compare and contrast.

QUARTERBACKS OF COLOR

It wasn't until 1968 that a person of color, Marlon Briscoe of the Denver Broncos, started as quarterback for an NFL franchise. Why? The answer appears to be ignorance and insensitivity. NFL coaches and executives actually believed that people of color couldn't process fast enough all the information a QB would need to succeed. It wasn't the first time a prejudice such as this had occurred in sports. When a basketball team representing the South Philadelphia Hebrew Association dominated in the 1920s, the press suggested in numerous articles that Jews were predisposed genetically to be superior basketball players.

As far as football is concerned, quarterback Doug Williams eventually shattered that terrible racial myth by leading Washington to a dominating 42 to 10 victory over Denver in the 1988 Super Bowl. He was the first African American quarterback to start in a Super Bowl and was named the game's MVP.

(19)

SCIENCE FICTION FRANCHISE

Star Trek vs. Star Wars

Science fiction has really evolved over time. Novels like Mary Shelley's *Frankenstein* (1918), Jules Verne's *Journey to the Center of the Earth* (1864) and *Twenty Thousand Leagues under the Sea* (1869), and H. G. Wells's *The War of the Worlds* (1898) paved the way to wide acceptance of the genre. The *Flash Gordon* TV series (1954) helped introduce rockets and space travel. The long-running British TV series *Dr. Who* (1963–present) emphasized traveling in time. These creations are the foundation upon which modern science fiction is built and owes a debt of gratitude. With so many different venues for entertainment today, choosing the G.O.A.T. in this category means examining franchises with multiple assortments of characters, often living in varying eras or even centuries, and having different story lines for TV, movies, and other types of media. The two heavyweights here are obviously *Star Trek* and *Star Wars*, each with their own passionate allegiance of fans. So rev your engines to either warp speed or hyperdrive and let the debate begin!

STAR TREK

Star Trek, the original TV series, debuted in September 1966 and ran for three seasons on NBC. That's right, just three seasons. It didn't

Star Trek. NBC/Photofest© NBC.

matter that the crew of the starship USS *Enterprise*, commanded by Captain James Tiberius Kirk (actor William Shatner), was on a "five-year mission to explore strange new worlds, to seek out new life and new civilizations, to boldly go where no man has gone before." The series was cancelled because of less than stellar ratings and high production costs. But as soon as it went into reruns, both in the United States and abroad, it built a cultlike following around the world. The fans who loved the series and its futuristic story lines and gadgets called themselves "Trekkies." The original series, set in the mid-twenty-second century, not only pushed the limits of time and space but also of social boundaries. The series was one of the first to ever have an interracial, on-screen kiss. Forced to do so by an alien's power of telekinesis (moving things with your mind), Captain Kirk kisses his communications officer Lt. Uhura, a Black woman portrayed by actress Nichelle Nichols. Kirk's essential crew was multiracial and also included Mr. Sulu, who was Asian, and Mr. Spock, a logic-driven alien with pointed ears from the planet Vulcan.

"Star Trek was an attempt to say that humanity will reach maturity and wisdom on the day that it begins not just to tolerate, but take a special delight in differences in ideas and differences in life forms," said its creator Gene Roddenberry. "If we cannot learn to actually enjoy those small differences, to take a positive delight in those small differences between our own kind, here on this planet, then we do not deserve to go out into space and meet the diversity that is almost certainly out there."[1]

Observing the success of *Star Wars*, Paramount Pictures produced thirteen *Star Trek* films, with the first six being based on the original series. The *Star Trek* franchise proved that it wasn't bound by its original characters. How do you rival an incredible lead character like Captain Kirk? Create one who is seemingly just the opposite. That's what *Star Trek: The Next Generation*, set in the twenty-fourth century, did in giving fans Captain Jean-Luc Picard. Portrayed by English actor Patrick Stewart, the bald-headed Picard was older than Kirk, far less physical and more cerebral in his approach to the part. Yet Trekkies still embraced him. Of course, there are several other successful incarnations of the franchise as well. Among them are *Deep Space Nine*, *Voyager*, *Enterprise*, *Discovery*, and *Picard*. Some of the

Actress Nichelle Nichols wanted to leave her role as Lt. Uhura on *Star Trek* to pursue a career on the Broadway stage. What changed her mind? She was told that a fan wanted to meet her. It turned out to be Dr. Martin Luther King Jr. The civil rights leader praised her as being one of the few TV role models for African Americans, in a time period when they mostly played subservient parts. He also told her that *Star Trek* was one of the few shows he'd let his children watch, because of the part she played. That meeting with King convinced Nichols to remain.

most memorable of the franchise's characters also include Scotty, Dr. "Bones" McCoy, Data, Worf, Geordi La Forge, Quark, Captain Janeway, and Seven of Nine.

STAR WARS

How iconic is the *Star Wars* film franchise? The first several seconds of the opening installment, *Star Wars: Episode IV—A New Hope* (1977), changed the face of film forever with the words, "In a galaxy far, far, away," slowly scrolling up the screen. Heroic characters such as Luke Skywalker, spiral-haired Princess Leia, Han Solo, and the woolly Chewbacca captured the imagination of audiences worldwide. C-3PO and R2-D2 connected to people on a very human level, despite both of them being droids. "The Force," an integral part of a new universe, found its way into the lexicon with the phrase, "May the Force be with you." There were light sabers, rebel forces, storm troopers, and a Jedi Knight named Obi-Wan Kenobi. And just when an audience couldn't be any more involved, there came the ominous presence of the mechanical-breathing Darth Vader, lord of the Dark Side. That's all from a single film, one generating a tsunami of science fiction creations that washed over our culture.

The very next episode, *The Empire Strikes Back* (1980), kept the franchise's momentum going. That film gave us Yoda, controlled and voiced by muppeteer Frank Oz. Size truly didn't matter for the diminutive green Jedi master of an unknown species who is virtually at one with the Force. Yoda even had his own style of speech that many tried

**Yoda from *Star Wars*. Lucasfilm Ltd./20th Century Fox/Photofest ©
Lucasfilm, Ltd.**

to emulate. *Speak like me, you try.* Then came the iconic line from the helmeted Darth Vader (voiced by actor James Earl Jones) uttered to Luke Skywalker at the climax of a light saber duel: "I am your father."

Star Wars was created and directed by filmmaker George Lucas.

"The secret to the movie business, or any business, is to get a good education in a subject besides film—whether it's history, psychology, economics, or architecture—so you have something to make a movie about. All the skill in the world isn't going to help you unless you have something to say," noted Lucas. "When I was making Star Wars, I wasn't restrained by any kind of science. I simply said, 'I'm going to create a world that's fun and interesting, makes sense, and seems to have a reality to it.'"[2]

After the release of the third installment, *Return of the Jedi* (1983), moviegoers learned about "prequels," as Lucas went back to before the beginning of his universe. The very first installment had been subtly labeled *IV*, giving Lucas license to provide audiences the opening prequel trilogy—*The Phantom Menace*, *Attack of the Clones*, and *Return of the Sith*. After that, Lucas rendered the remaining episodes—*The Force Awakens VII*, *The Last Jedi VIII*, and *The Rise of Skywalker IX*. They were a collection of nine films that changed the way we relate to science fiction. "I'll never turn to the Dark Side," Luke Skywalker assures us. And we absolutely believe him.

TIME TO DEBATE

Which would you choose as the G.O.A.T. of sci-fi franchises, *Star Trek* or *Star Wars*? Possibly you have a different franchise or even a single series in mind. Remember, yesterday's science fiction can easily become tomorrow's reality. Maybe you'll influence the future world in some way too, either by what you think or something you create, much like Gene Roddenberry and George Lucas. To that end, for a debate topic such as sci-fi franchises, don't be afraid to use your imagination to further your position. Since it is already fiction, you could easily insert yourself or the listener into the argument for emphasis. That would be one way to highlight your point of view.

Debater #1: "I would definitely be more excited to fight alongside Luke Skywalker with a light saber than Captain Kirk with a phaser. Wouldn't you?"

Debater #2: "Being the future captain of the USS Enterprise *and giving the command to travel at warp-speed has long been a dream of mine. Maybe you've had that same ambition."*

LIGHTNING DEBATE

Which alien do you think your parents would be more comfortable hosting for dinner, *Star Trek*'s Mr. Spock with his Vulcan logic or *Star Wars*'s diminutive Force-wielding Yoda? We can't wait to hear your reasoning.

FROM SCI-FI TO REALITY

Plenty of science fiction writers have correctly foreseen the future. 3-D printers or "replicators" are discussed in an episode of *Star Trek*, almost two decades before the first working version of one was manufactured.[3] Though current models of hoverboards don't actually fly (but instead self-balance), they were initially conceived of by author M. K. Joseph in his 1967 novel, *The Hole in the Zero*. In the novel *Fahrenheit 451* (1953), author Ray Bradbury envisions cities of people walking around with earbud-like devices, each listening to their own music. Douglas Adams's *The Hitchhikers' Guide to the Galaxy* (1978) features Babel Fish, which work as universal translators, much like today's audio-translation apps, allowing those speaking different languages to instantly be understood.

20

SCIENTIST

Marie Curie vs. Albert Einstein

Perhaps science is your favorite subject. You feel passionate about it, and maybe you even consider yourself a scientist. There have been many people, though, who have been completely consumed by science—doctors, chemists, researchers, biologists, ecologists, and many more. Ask your science teacher why they chose to dedicate their professional life to the subject. I'm sure they'll tell you that there's even a higher level of dedication by a select group of people who think, eat, and breathe science 24/7. Those are the types of scientists we considered in selecting the G.O.A.T.

MARIE CURIE (1867–1934)

"Nothing in life is to be feared, it is only to be understood. Now is the time to understand more, so that we may fear less." —M. C.

Marie Curie was born in Warsaw, Poland, when it was under the oppressive control of the Russian Empire. Universities there didn't allow women to enroll, and Curie's parents didn't have the money to send Marie and her sisters abroad to study. There were, however, secret schools for women called "flying universities" or "floating universities." Marie built upon her basic education in such places. Only she wanted much more. How did Marie Curie ultimately receive the higher education to allow her incredible scientific mind to develop? It happened through a combination of family, sacrifice, and trust. She made a pact with one of her sisters. Marie would work as a governess (taking care of other people's children) for the two years it would take her sister to graduate from a medical school in Paris. All of the money Marie earned would go to finance her sister's tuition. Once her sister graduated and began working, her sister's money would then go toward Marie's tuition. It didn't all go smoothly. It was a difficult struggle for both sisters. But their plan ultimately succeeded.[1]

"Life is not easy for any of us. . . . We must have perseverance and above all confidence in ourselves. We must believe that we are gifted for something, and that this thing, at whatever cost, must be attained," said Curie.[2]

As a physicist, Marie's mind was intrigued by strange substances that glowed when exposed to bright light (X-rays had only recently been discovered). She focused on an element called thorium and learned that it wasn't the arrangement of atoms that made it radiate (give off light) but the interior of the atom itself. Scientists around the globe were awed by her ingenious discovery. Along with her husband, Pierre, Marie spent hundreds of grueling hours separating the elements in acid until she'd extracted a black powder three hundred times more radioactive than uranium. She called the element "polonium," named after her native Poland. This theory of "radioactivity" earned Marie Curie a Nobel Prize in Physics, making her the first woman to ever win a Nobel Prize. Several years later, after the death of her husband, Marie Curie won a Nobel Prize in Chemistry, in part for her isolation of radium from both uranium and thorium. She is the only person to win Nobel Prizes in two different fields.[3]

Tragically for Marie Curie, it was not known at the time that radioactive substances were extremely damaging to healthy tissues. Her long-term exposure to these substances was the cause of her death. Even Curie's scientific papers, which had become radioactive, are stored in a lead-lined box to protect others.

ALBERT EINSTEIN (1879–1955)

The scientific prowess of Albert Einstein is thoroughly ingrained into our society. How much so? If you were doing something remarkably intelligent, it wouldn't be uncommon for someone to yell at you, *"Hey, Einstein!"*

Albert Einstein. *Associated Press/Photofest ©Associated Press.*

There are several myths about Einstein, including that he failed mathematics in school. That's untrue. As a youngster, the German-born physicist was intrigued by invisible forces in the natural world, like the way a compass needle always points toward magnetic north. Einstein's scientific discoveries would eventually redefine the way we perceive space, time, matter, energy, and gravity.

"I have no special talents. I am only passionately curious," said Einstein.[4]

For example, he taught us that light consists of small particles called photons. But that light needs to be considered as both a particle and a wave. Though neither the particle nor wave view gives us a complete picture of light on its own—together, they do. That was the start of a field called quantum mechanics.

Einstein also clued us in to the concept of black holes. It starts with the gravitational attraction between large bodies, warping time and space. That produces a region of space where the gravitational attraction is so strong that even light cannot escape.[5] Then there's his famous equation: $E=mc^2$. Seemingly, everyone's heard of it. But what exactly does it mean? The equation is a result of Einstein's theory of special relativity, which states that mass and energy are the same physical entity and can be changed into each other. Even today, it remains our most accurate model of motion at any speed, including bodies approaching the speed of light. The theory also implies that gravity has the ability to bend light and could be used to calculate the amount of energy released during nuclear reactions.

Einstein's discoveries were the beginning of nuclear energy and, sadly, nuclear weapons. Though Einstein was a pacifist and hated violence, he understood that Nazi Germany, from where he'd become a refugee because of his Jewish heritage, couldn't be the first to develop an atomic bomb. So he urged the United States, in a 1939 letter to President Franklin Delano Roosevelt, to win the race to possess such a devastating weapon in what would be called the "Manhattan Project."[6] The United States ultimately used this weapon to end World War II, leaving generations of people affected by the bombing of Hiroshima in Japan.

"A human being is a part of the whole called by us universe, a part limited in time and space. He experiences himself, his thoughts and feeling as something separated from the rest, a kind of optical delusion of his consciousness. This delusion is a kind of prison for us, restricting us to our personal desires and to affection for a few persons nearest to us," said Einstein. "Our task must be to free ourselves from this prison by widening our circle of compassion to embrace all living creatures and the whole of nature in its beauty."[7]

Einstein's theories have also been the cornerstone of modern technologies such as computers and GPS satellites. Because of his outstanding contributions to the world, *Time* magazine named Albert Einstein its Person of the Century.

THE LETTER

You've probably heard of cyberbullying and the damage it can cause to people. Before the internet, newspapers and journals were where the bullies of earlier times tossed their spiked barbs at others. Marie Curie was bullied in the press. It seems that after her husband died, she began a relationship with a man who was still legally married to someone else. In response, many in the scientific community said some nasty things about her in the press in an effort to hurt her credibility as a scientist. Was she being treated differently because she was a woman? Albert Einstein was angry at the treatment Marie Curie incurred. So he sent her the letter (1911) below:

Highly esteemed Mrs. Curie,

Do not laugh at me for writing you without having anything sensible to say. But I am so enraged by the base manner in which the public is presently daring to concern itself with you that I absolutely must give vent to this feeling. However, I am convinced that you consistently despise this rabble, whether it obsequiously lavishes respect on you or whether it attempts to satiate its lust for sensationalism! I am impelled to tell you how much I have come to admire your intellect, your drive, and your honesty, and that I consider myself lucky to have made your personal acquaintance in Brussels. Anyone who does not number among these reptiles is certainly happy, now as before, that we have such personages among us as you, . . . If the rabble continues to occupy itself with you, then simply don't read that hogwash, but rather leave it to the reptile for whom it has been fabricated.

With most amicable regards to you . . . yours very truly,
Einstein

Who's the greatest scientist of all time? Is it one of our presented choices: Marie Curie or Albert Einstein? There are many others who have made outstanding contributions to the field of science. Maybe you'd like to choose someone else and write their entry yourself. It would certainly make a marvelous debate in any school science class.

TIME TO DEBATE

There's a famous saying—*it's the message not the medium*. That simply means what you say (the message) is more important than the means (the medium) by which you deliver it. However, that notion got turned upside down during the first 1960 presidential debate between John F. Kennedy and Richard Nixon. Most people who heard the debate on the radio thought both candidates gave a good account of themselves. But a majority of people who'd watched the debate on television, which was new to many households at the time, came away with the opinion that Kennedy was the winner. Why? Kennedy stared straight into the camera when answering questions, while Nixon looked off to the side at reporters. Compared to Kennedy, Nixon had a pale complexion and wore a gray suit which blended into the debate's background. He'd also been suffering from a mild flu and campaigned all day prior to the debate. Meanwhile, Kennedy had been resting most of the afternoon, prepping for the debate in his hotel room. Consequently, Nixon appeared tired and gaunt compared to the bronze-skinned Kennedy. Did the visuals make a difference? Less than four months later, Kennedy edged Nixon in the presidential election by 13,000 (popular) votes, an ultraslim margin of 1.7 percent.[8]

(21)

STUNT PERSON

Dar Robinson vs. Jeannie Epper

Could be you've taken a heart-stopping fall in your life—off of a bicycle, skateboard, or maybe even a horse. It probably wasn't planned. But if you felt a rush of adrenaline in mid-fall, almost as if you were enjoying it, then it's possible you might one day have a career in stunts. It isn't easy to figure out who's the greatest stunt person of all time. Most stunt people don't get star billing, even though they might be responsible for the most exciting scenes in a TV show or movie. Instead of craving attention from the public, stunt people are usually satisfied by the recognition of their peers. For our purposes, however, we'll put the names of a pair of renowned stunt people front and center on a brightly lit marquee—Dar Robinson and Jeannie Epper.

DAR ROBINSON (1947–1986)

As a young kid in California, Dar Robinson spent thousands of hours on the trampoline honing his acrobatic skills. By the time he was twenty-one, Robinson was working on Hollywood film sets performing stunts or gags. Over his long career, he became known as "The Ultimate Stuntman," because of his ability to conceive difficult, eye-catching stunts, as well as to execute them with the view of the audience in mind. To this end, Robinson invented the decelerator (drag-line cables) so that he could leap from a tall height, usually off of a building. Thus, the camera could shoot the stunt from the top down, because there was no immense air bag to be seen on the ground to break his fall. There was only a one-eighth-inch thick cable, thin enough so that the camera couldn't see it. That cable was connected to his chest and ankle, which first slowed him down and then stopped his fall approximately ten feet from the ground. In 1979, Robinson used his decelerator to leap from the seven-hundred foot tall CN Tower in Toronto, Canada for the film *Highpoint*.

Robinson was the holder of twenty-one world stunt records, and in his first nineteen years as a stuntman he didn't break a single bone in his body.

"I am afraid of almost all of the work that I do," said Robinson, who possessed tremendous powers of concentration. "Anyone who says they're not afraid is either foolish or crazy."[1]

Sadly, Dar Robinson was killed on a movie set while making a high-speed run past the camera on a motorcycle. He missed the braking point on a turn and his motorcycle plunged off a cliff.[2]

JEANNIE EPPER (B. 1941)

Legendary stuntwoman Jeannie Epper has appeared in over one hundred films and television shows. She is probably best known for being Lynda Carter's stunt double on the superhero-genre TV show *Wonder Woman*. She also did incredible and death-defying stunts in the films *Romancing the Stone* and *Kill Bill Volume II*. But maybe the most amazing thing about Jeannie Epper is that she continues to work at this ultrademanding profession as she approaches the age of eighty.

"I like the adventure, the adrenaline, being able to do things a normal person can't do. I've never been scared, but I've always had respect for the stunt," said Epper.[3]

She started at age eighteen with a saddle-fall from a fast-moving horse, quickly becoming a student of how stunts could be done more safely, measuring them out in her mind to the last inch. If Epper believed there was too little margin for error, she would be the first to argue with her bosses on how to change the dynamics of the stunt to make it safer. Don't misunderstand; Epper has performed some immensely dangerous gags such as swinging across a ravine on a vine and careening down a steep hill amid an orchestrated mudslide, over and over until it looked perfect on camera.

The rise of more women starring in action roles opened up the industry to stuntwomen. Epper, whose father was also a stunt performer, rode that new wave of opportunities during the 1970s. She not only broke the glass ceiling for women in the stunt industry, but on camera, she literally crashed through it as well.

Epper was given the Artemis Stunt Lifetime Achievement Award for her amazing five decades as a stuntwoman, stunt driver, and stunt coordinator—the first woman to receive the award.

"It isn't just about stunts. It's about who you are as a person," emphasized Epper.[4]

Maybe there's some incredible stunt scene in a movie or TV show that you can't get out of your mind. It probably wasn't the actor or actress in the starring role performing it, but rather a stunt double. Go to the production's credits and find out who really made that memorable impression on you. You could even debate that person's merits as possibly the greatest stunt performer of all time.

TIME TO DEBATE

The key to being a stunt performer is to be both relaxed and prepared. That's exactly what it takes to be a good debater. Being relaxed as a speaker comes with practice. So the more you speak in public, the less stress you will feel while arguing your position in front of an audience. We've previously discussed practicing in front of a mirror. Your family and friends can also be a good first audience for you.

Preparation is also a key element. The more you've prepared, the easier debating becomes. Having your position, reasons, facts, and counterarguments committed to memory is the best way to keep a natural flow, be less tense, and ultimately be more successful.

(22)

SUPERHERO SQUAD

Justice League vs. Avengers

Who better to solve the problems of the world than a superhero, even if most of these same cape-wearing wonders can't solve the problems in their own lives? But what happens if the disaster gets so big or the villains so powerful that a single superhero can't get the job done alone? Well, that's why we have superhero squads, where the individual, no matter how singularly powerful, relies on the help of others. So who's the G.O.A.T. of superhero teamwork—D.C. Comics's Justice League or Marvel Comics's Avengers?

JUSTICE LEAGUE

Born in 1960, and conceived of by comic strip creator Gardner Fox, D.C. Comics's Justice League (originally called Justice League of America) was comprised of seven superheroes. They are Superman, Batman, Wonder Woman, Flash, Green Lantern, Aquaman, and Martian Manhunter. Here's the scouting report: this squad has speed (Flash), strength (Superman), the ability to make their adversaries tell the truth (Wonder Woman's Golden Lasso), and the world's greatest martial artist (Batman), for starters. Which unstoppable villain caused

the team to first join forces? Was it a large-brained humanoid with
the ability to plan incredibly complicated attacks on mankind? Could
it have been a savage fire-breathing monster that crushed skyscrapers
by simply stamping them with its enormous feet? No. It was a starfish from space called Starro the Conqueror. That's right, a starfish.
Don't laugh, though. Starro did infect Earth's native starfish, bringing
together a small army of the five-tentacle creatures that absorbed the
energy from an exploded nuclear bomb and even practiced mind-
control over humans while capturing a pair of cities.[1]

The Justice League appropriately calls the Hall of Justice their
headquarters. Located in Washington, DC, the Hall of Justice was
designed by Wonder Woman and architect John Stewart, DC Comics's first black superhero who became one of the Green Lanterns. It
was then financed by Batman, aka millionaire Bruce Wayne, and built
from scratch by Superman.[2]

If you're a fan of Marvel Comics's The Fantastic Four (comprised
of Mr. Fantastic, Invisible Girl, Human Torch, and Ben Grimm as
the stony strongman Thing), you really have the Justice League to
thank. Marvel Comics asked Spiderman creator Stan Lee to develop
the Fantastic Four because the Justice League was selling so many
comic books.[3]

Over its six decades of existence, the Justice League, whose cast
of characters has changed slightly at various times, has spawned animated TV shows, movies, video games, and even rides at theme parks,
which often feature a life-size Hall of Justice. A word of advice—don't
take the seat next to Aquaman at the Hall of Justice's meeting table.
Why? We always find him a little fishy.

AVENGERS

Created by Stan Lee and Jack Kirby, the Avengers debuted in a 1963
comic. They were billed as "Earth's Mightiest Heroes." That was
probably a direct slap by Marvel at DC's Justice League. Were these
comic companies really run by adults? The original Avengers con-
sisted of a pentagon of heroes; Iron Man (in a completely yellow/gold
suit with no red trim), Wasp, Hulk, Thor, and Ant Man. They were

eventually joined by Steve Rogers, aka Captain America, after he was rescued from being trapped in ice and in suspended animation since his fight against the Nazis nearing the end of World War II. Here's the Avengers scouting report: they can go big or small with Hulk at one end of the spectrum while Ant Man and Wasp occupy the other. Tony Stark (Iron Man) is a wealthy weapons inventor, and Steve Rogers received a supersoldier serum (an early version of steroids) to enhance him both physically and mentally. And, of course, Thor is an Asgardian god. Do I need to say anything more? He's a god!

What supervillain first brought the Avengers together? It was Thor's self-serving brother Loki, who used the unwitting Hulk as a pawn to seek revenge against Thor. That rallied Ant Man, Wasp, and Iron Man to come to their aid. It was Ant Man who suggested the heroes form a team and coined the name "Avengers." What's the rallying cry they use to bring the team together in times of trouble? It's "Avengers Assemble!"

The group meets in the Avengers' Mansion, which has an actual address—890 Fifth Avenue in New York City's borough of Manhattan. Does that address actually exist? Yes. It is the Henry Clay Frick House, which is currently a museum displaying art and architecture. Stan Lee saw the building every day on his commute to work and made it part of the Avengers' history (in the story line it belongs to Tony Stark).[4] The Avengers even have a butler, Edwin Jarvis, in the mansion to tend to their needs.

In 1971, Marvel Comics took another not-so-subtle swipe at the Justice League when it created Squadron Sinister for the Avengers to battle. The characters are clearly based on their superhero rivals: Hyperion/Superman, Nighthawk/Batman, Power Princess/Wonder Woman, Doctor Spectrum/Green Lantern, and Speed Demon/Flash. They are their evil counterparts.

There's little doubt that the Avengers have the edge over Justice League when it comes to major motion pictures. There have been four blockbuster films with "Avengers" in the title, not counting the spin-offs for Hulk, Iron Man, Captain America, Ant Man, and Wasp. There is just a single flick with "Justice League" in the title. By the way, comic book companies never used the word "flick" in place of "movie." Why? They were afraid the ink would accidentally run, melding the L and I together to form an expletive (profanity) for which they could be heavily fined.

Who's your choice for the greatest superhero team of all time—Justice League or Avengers? Perhaps you're a fan of Teen Titans, Guardians of the Galaxy, League of Extraordinary Gentlemen, X-Men, or some other squad. The debate is ready to begin between you and your friends. And maybe even with several of your super-hero-worshipping teachers.

TIME TO DEBATE

Here's a pair of key words for winning arguments or debates—"refute" or "refutation." That means disproving the other side's coun-terargument against your position. It's like the counterpunching our superhero squads use against the attacks of various villains. Below are two examples of how it's done verbally.

Debater #1: "My opponent's idea that the Justice League's power starts and ends with Superman is insulting to the rest of that squad. To illustrate my point, Wonder Woman alone has saved mankind on numerous occasions . . ."

Debater #2: "My opponent states that the Avengers are a copycat of Justice League. But the Avengers have broken new ground for a superhero squad in many ways. For example, as a team they have . . ."

LIGHTNING DEBATE

There's a drought in California, and the southern part of the state desperately needs rain. Imagine you could bring the superheroes to life. Who would do a better job of causing several inches of precipita-tion in a targeted area—Superman or Thor? We know the reasoning supporting your choice will be spot-on.

COMICS, MYTHS, AND BOOKS

Comics often use literature for their inspiration. The Justice League meets around a large circular table in the Hall of Justice. That was most likely inspired by the legend of King Arthur and his Knights of the Round Table. Thor is based on the mythological Norse God of Thunder and his mighty hammer, *Mjolnir*, which produces a thunderous sound when struck. Characters that inhabit his world such as Odin and Loki come from the same myths. The Hulk, who is mild-mannered Dr. Bruce Banner when he is not enraged, comes directly from the gothic novella by Scottish author Robert Louis Stevenson titled *Dr. Jekyll and Mr. Hyde*, in which the main character also transforms into a creature with anger issues.

23

TV MOMENT

Moon Landing vs. Ellen's Coming-out Episode

One of the ways our society bonds is through the moments we share together. TV has been an incredibly important part of that societal cohesiveness. Images and audio broadcasts provide us with a common starting point, even if our ultimate conclusion about the events we've viewed differs. There have been thousands of such moments since the mid-1950s, when the majority of US households purchased their first TV. But what is the greatest TV moment of all time? Is it comedic, like Lucille Ball standing at the end of a conveyor belt as the chocolates start to come faster and faster? Is it tragic like the Space Shuttle *Challenger* disintegrating before our eyes just after its launch and ending the lives of all seven souls on board? It was a difficult decision. But of the pair we've chosen for our upcoming debate—one moment is triumphant, while the other denotes a marker of change and acceptance in our society.

MOON LANDING (1969)

> *"It suddenly struck me that that tiny pea, pretty and blue, was the Earth. I put up my thumb and shut one eye, and my thumb blotted out the planet Earth. I didn't feel like a giant. I felt very, very small."* —N. A.

On July 20, 1969, the perceived boundaries of our earthly limitations changed forever when astronaut Neal Armstrong set foot upon the moon. That historic change was delivered worldwide via TV at 10:56 p.m. ET. The Apollo 11 *Eagle* spacecraft had a small camera mounted on its side. The grainy transmission sent back to earth was viewed by hundreds of millions of people at the apex of a thirty-hour broadcast. Famed news anchor Walter Cronkite was almost left speechless in the studio, simply uttering, "Man on the moon . . . Oh, boy . . . Whew, boy." Thankfully, Armstrong provided us with something more poetic and profound to ponder when he said, "That's one small step for man, one giant leap for mankind."

That televised event also declared the United States a winner in the space race against Russia—part of a Cold War skirmish to see who could reach the moon first.[1]

Broadcasting through deep space wasn't easy with the technology available at the time. NASA (National Air and Space Agency), though, wasn't about to let the publicity/celebration of live visuals from the moon slip away. A special lunar camera had to be designed to meet a demanding set of circumstances—sudden weightlessness, substantial temperature differences in space, and the contrast between a bright lunar surface and the atmosphere-less black sky.

The US Department of Defense allowed the Apollo 11 mission to use secretive technology developed for wartime, when a pilot downed behind enemy lines might need to see at night. The one-of-a-kind camera was covered by a thermal blanket with just the lens peeking through.[2] Buzz Aldrin was the second astronaut to leave the module and walk the surface of the moon. The final member of the three-man crew, pilot Michael Collins, remained inside the spacecraft.

The immense audience watched in awe as the pair of astronauts erected a US flag, collected soil samples, moon rocks, and used a Kangaroo-style hop to move about in an atmosphere with only one-sixth the gravity of earth.

How can we properly frame TV's role in this monumental event?

"It took place 238,000 miles out in space, yet it was shared by hundreds of millions of people on earth," said Richard Salant, the president of CBS News at the time. "The step on the moon was an awesome achievement; so was its reporting on television because it emphasized television's extraordinary ability to unify a disparate world through communicating with so many people, in so many places, and thus providing them with a common—and an extraordinarily satisfying—experience. . . . (It) ranks as the single most satisfying effort in our collective experience as journalists. All too often, we are forced to report man's shortcomings. In this instance, from the moment of blast-off to the moment of splashdown we were continually conscious of being involved in one of the great triumphs of the human spirit."[3]

ELLEN'S COMING-OUT EPISODE (1997)

Today, maybe it doesn't seem like an earth-shattering event for a character in an ultrapopular sitcom to announce that he or she is gay. But just a few decades ago, such topics weren't explored. That is until comedian/actress Ellen DeGeneres did it on the ABC-TV sitcom *Ellen*. What made the bold step even more personal was that DeGeneres was playing the show's main protagonist, Ellen Morgan, a character named and fashioned after herself. So the announcement actually proclaimed to the world two things: both Ellen Morgan (the character) and Ellen DeGeneres (the sitcom's star) were coming out of the closet together and publicly joining the LGBTQ community.

The "Coming-out" episode aired on April 30, 1997. One week prior, DeGeneres appeared on the cover of *Time* magazine with a headline reading: "Yep, I'm Gay." The episode, which was expanded to a full hour from its usual half-hour format, drew a staggering forty-two million viewers.[4] Many people watched waiting to applaud the program's resolution, while others tuned in solely to condemn the content. Of course, the buildup to the episode also inspired a pro- and con-public debate, which intensified the closer it came to airing. ABC received a ton of complaints and hate mail. Talk-radio hosts and televangelists with a differing point of view than Ellen's began to refer to her as "Ellen DeGenerate" and blasted the upcoming episode as a "blatant attempt to promote homosexuality." Some advertisers, fearing a potential backlash on their products, pulled their ads from the episode.

In response to the negative voices, DeGeneres said, "I had no idea the amount of hate. I had no idea that there would be death threats or a bomb scare. It was a really scary time."[5]

In support of Ellen, however, many Hollywood stars and entertainers—such as Oprah Winfrey, who played Ellen's therapist—asked to be included in the episode to show their public support.

How does the truth slip out on camera? In a crowded airport, Ellen, in an emotional conversation with a woman with whom she'd like to start a relationship (Susan, played by actress Laura Dern) said, "I'm thirty-five years old. I'm so afraid to tell people. I'm just . . . Susan [Ellen leans closer to her, inadvertently hovering over a live microphone at the airline boarding counter] . . . I'm gay" (her voice amplified throughout the airport).

"At the time, it was so controversial. . . . It was (on paper) called *The Puppy Episode* until it aired because *Ellen Throws Her Career Away* seemed too on the nose. [And] when the writers told the executives they wanted me to 'come out' because my character needed to be in a relationship . . . someone at the studio said 'Get her a puppy because she's not coming out'. . . . I can't describe to you how challenging it was to get this episode made," said DeGeneres in 2017, while celebrating the episode's twentieth anniversary.[6]

Many TV shows since have featured LGBTQ characters. Sitcoms such as *Glee*, *Modern Family*, and *Will & Grace* all had the landscape paved for them by that singular episode of *Ellen*.

In 2016, DeGeneres received the Medal of Freedom from President Barack Obama, in part, for her participation in that episode. "At a pivotal moment, her courage and candor helped change the minds of millions of Americans, accelerating our nation's constant drive toward equality and acceptance for all," remarked Obama.

TIME TO DEBATE

There have been many historic TV moments besides the pair that we've chosen to debate. You most likely have several that hold great meaning to your own life. We challenge you to turn to someone with whom you watch TV regularly, maybe a family member, and ask them to search their memories for the G.O.A.T. of TV moments. Do they deal with sports? Entertainment? News? Perhaps you could have a spirited household debate on this subject using and sharing the techniques you've learned in this book.

24

VIDEO GAME

Mario Brothers vs. Pac-Man

The first video game to capture the world's imagination was Atari's *Pong* (1972). It was a table tennis game containing bare-bones graphics—straight white lines and a scoreboard. It was only the beginning, though. The 1980s brought 8-bit graphics and the emergence of character-driven games for companies like Sega, Nintendo, and Coleco. What's the greatest video game of all time? Well, can old-school video games really compete with today's amazing graphics and high-tech industry advances, such as virtual gaming? We think they can because our pair of entries for this category definitely has an old-school feel to it. So go grab a game pad or even an old-fashioned joystick and join the debate.

MARIO BROTHERS

It's hard to believe that a pair of fictitious Italian-American plumbers, brothers named Mario and Luigi, could change the way people relate to video games. But it happened. Nintendo, a Japanese gaming company, first marketed *Mario Brothers* in 1983. It sold fewer than four thousand arcade cabinets in the United States. The real revolution didn't come in arcades where patrons fed quarters into a slot. Instead, the story-based video game exploded in the brand-new home market where people, and more importantly families, played for hours at a time, sitting comfortably on their living room couch. The *Mario Brothers* game cartridge for Atari and NES sold nearly four million copies worldwide.[1]

Mario Brothers was created by famed designer Shigeru Miyamoto, who is also responsible for *Donkey Kong* (where Mario made his first appearance) and *The Legend of Zelda*. Miyamoto's plumbers weren't there to simply achieve a high score. Rather, players moved their characters in a linear fashion across a virtual stage of lands and levels by running, jumping, and dodging both obstacles and adversaries.

"Players are artists who create their own reality within the game," said Miyamoto, whom *Time* magazine called the (Steven) Spielberg of video games. "When I'm working on games I don't think necessarily about what the end benefit of the game is going to be. Typically I'm trying to think—what can I do that is going to find new ways to entertain and surprise people."[2]

In 1985, *Super Mario Brothers* hit the market, franchising the characters and expanding their world (there are eight worlds, each comprised of four levels). Miyamoto's fantasy story of the Mushroom Kingdom attacked by turtle-like creatures called Koopa Troopas wholly resonated with players. The chief villain in the game is Bowser, King of the Koopas. This fire-breathing spiked-shelled turtle has used his evil sorcery to kidnap Princess Peach and turn the inhabitants of the kingdom into inanimate objects, such as bricks and coins. Mario is quested to rescue the princess and must face Bowser one-on-one in the final level to achieve that goal.

Mario-mania didn't stop there. Mario is either the main character or a supporting cast member in approximately one hundred video games. A few of the more popular versions are Mario Kart (go-cart racing), Paper Mario, and Super Mario Sunshine. There's even a video game where Mario can teach you how to type. Mario is the official mascot of Nintendo. Since 1990, the character has been voiced by Charles Martinet, who was intent on giving his version of Mario a "more soft-hearted and friendly" tone than the somewhat harsher original. In his mind, Martinet based the voice on the character Petruchio in Shakespeare's play *The Taming of the Shrew*. And no, Petruchio is not an Elizabethan plumber. He is described as a "fortune seeker." Charles Martinet also voices Mario's brother, Luigi. After all, they are fraternal twins.[3]

PAC-MAN

During the late 1970s, the dominant themes in video games were war and sports. Japanese game designer Toru Iwatani wanted something different. He was searching for a game that would appeal to as many women as men. In 1980, he came up with the idea of *Pac-Man* for a gaming company called Namco. It was a maze arcade game in which a character, Pac-Man, shaped like a pizza with a slice missing to resemble a mouth, ate energy pellets while being chased by a quartet of ghostlike characters.

Perhaps the most exciting moment of the game comes when Pac-Man eats a flashing energy pellet. That gives Pac-Man the power to vanquish the ghosts. So the chased or hunted character suddenly becomes the hunter. That boost of energy, however, doesn't last long. It's a challenge of time and space, negotiating the confines of the maze. Why is eating part of the concept? In looking for a theme with which both sexes could identify, Iwatani settled on food. He based the shape of his Pac-Man character on a more rounded version of "*Kuchi*," the Japanese symbol for the word mouth.[4] Originally, the character was named Puck-Man (like a hockey puck). But Iwatani was worried that it would be too tempting for vandals in US arcades to change the first letter, turning it into an expletive (profanity). Much to the designer's surprise, the game's Ghost Gang became beloved characters. Their names are Blinky (red), Pinky (pink), Inky (blue), and Clyde (orange).

"I had no special training at all. I am completely self-taught," said Iwatani. "I don't fit the mold of a visual arts designer or a graphic designer. I just had a strong concept about what a game designer is— someone who designs projects to make people happy. That's a game designer's purpose."[5]

Two years later, in keeping with the idea of creating video games that appealed to more women, Iwatani and Namco put out *Ms.*

Pac-Man, which was an instant success with gamers, both male and female. There's also *Pac-Man Jr.* and *Baby Pac-Man* as part of the family and franchise. You say a video game designer had a part in a major motion picture? Yes. It happened in the 2015 film *Pixels*, about an alien race who believe our video games are real and how we settle conflicts on Earth. The aliens send a huge and hungry Pac-Man to satisfy his appetite on Manhattan. Creator Toru Iwatani is a character in the movie, though he does not play himself. Instead, he is portrayed by an actor. His character approaches the out-of-control Pac-Man. In a soothing voices he says, "I'm your father. I know you're a good boy." An instant later, Pac-Man chomps down his hand. The Iwatani-character runs in the opposite direction screaming, "Somebody kill that stupid thing!" Did we fail to mention that *Pixels* is a comedy?

There are many more incredible games worthy of consideration that we didn't discuss: Games like *Tetris*, a mathematically minded, multicolored tile-building game. *Tony Hawk's Pro Skater* allows you to skateboard like a pro without the skinned-knees. *Grand Theft Auto* (we endorse the game, not the criminal activity). *The Legend of Zelda* with its superb mix of puzzles and action-adventure. Or feel free to add your personal favorite to the debate for the G.O.A.T. of video games.

TIME TO DEBATE

C-SPAN was created in 1979 by the cable TV industry as a public service. The channel televises many congressional sessions of both the Senate and House of Representatives. Therefore, you will see many political debates on important issues of the day. If you're truly interested in building up your argumentative and debate skills, take note of the different styles used by the various speakers. Just remember, sometimes politicians break the rules of fair and reasonable debate. You might even hear them attacking their opponents instead of arguing the merits of their own position. Try not to fall into this trap yourself. It will only serve to lessen your stature as a speaker and simply shouldn't be part of any meaningful debate.

25

VILLAIN (FICTIONAL)

Lord Voldemort vs. Joker

You can praise your heroes from now until doomsday. But there probably wouldn't be any heroes, nor the possibility of an impending doomsday, without a villain to make us fearful. Who is the greatest fictional villain of all time? There are so many worthy choices in this category. That's because almost every incredible action story arises from the malicious deeds of one individual. Remember, the more fearsome the villain, the greater the tension felt by the audience. Unfortunately, our dark-sided debate will leave out some classic evil-doers including Freddy Krueger, Michael Myers, Thanos, Pennywise, Lex Luthor, Harley Quinn, Magneto, Green Goblin, Hannibal Lecter, Darth Vader, and even Bruce, the shark from the movie *Jaws*. However, the two we've presented below can get down and dirty with any of the aforementioned villains.

LORD VOLDEMORT

> *"There is no good and evil. There is only power . . . and those too weak to seek it."* —L. V.

What makes the Dark Lord among the most feared villains ever? Consider this—an entire culture of ultrapowerful wizards is basically petrified to string together the three syllables that comprise his name. When British author J. K. Rowling established her Harry Potter series's evil presence as "He-who-must-not-be-named," she fully realized the tension it would create. Eventually, we discover that Lord Voldemort—born Tom Marvolo Riddle, an anagram for Lord Voldemort—constructed his own name, after his human (Muggle) father left his wizard mother.

"I fashioned myself a new name. A name I knew wizards everywhere would one day fear to speak, when I had become the greatest sorcerer in the world!" said Voldemort.

Consequently, we feel that Voldemort is everywhere. He practically permeates every shadow and hidden crevice of the story. We don't even catch a glimpse of the Dark Lord until late in the first installment when he appears on the back of the head of a Hogwarts professor. Now that's an evil entrance to be remembered.

Voldemort doesn't regain his body until the fourth installment of the series, and we're still totally spooked by him. What about his physical appearance? Voldemort is both hairless and lipless. Rowling deftly describes her hideous villain as having pale skin, a skull-like face, snakelike slits for nostrils, red eyes and catlike slits for pupils, a skeletally thin body, and long, thin hands with unnaturally long fingers.

There is no redeeming value in Voldemort (unlike how Darth Vader eventually chose his son, Luke Skywalker, over the Dark Side and the Emperor). Voldemort's singular purpose is to kill Harry Potter. He even tried to murder Harry as a defenseless infant. That's the sign of an absolute coal-black heart.

Hatred is an essential part of a great villain, and Voldemort is filled with it to his core. The Dark Lord hates non-pureblood wizards. In actuality, that means he literally hates himself, which is always a fascinating facet of a monstrous evil-doer. He also commands a legion of terrorist followers called Death Eaters, who likewise despise Muggle-blooded wizards or anyone standing against their genocidal cause.

Lord Voldemort is frightfully talented at his craft. Despite not being exposed to magic until he was ten years old, he became the greatest student ever produced by the Hogwarts School of Witchcraft

Lord Voldemort. *Warner Bros./Photofest © Warner Bros.*

and Wizardry. He even receives the reluctant respect of Headmaster Dumbledore, who admits that Voldemort's brand of black magic is "more extensive than any wizard alive."[1] Of course, we hate Voldemort, not only because he wants to destroy our hero, but also because he murdered Harry's parents, making him an orphan. And the more Harry professes his love for his departed mother and father, the more we convulse at the thought of the superbly villainous Voldemort.

JOKER

> "We stopped checking for monsters under our bed, when we realized they were inside us." —J.

There have been many incarnations of the Joker—film, TV, and comic-book versions. But the green-haired, face-painted, sadistic madman has aced the test of time and easily risen to the height of becoming both Batman's and Gotham City's most feared archvillain. Created by Bill Finger, Bob Kane, and Jerry Robinson, Joker first appeared in a 1940 DC Comics' edition titled *Batman*. Several actors have portrayed the Joker character, rendering outstanding and disturbing

Joker. Warner Bros./Photofest© Warner Bros. Photographer: Stephen Vaughan.

performances. Those actors include Jack Nicholson, Heath Ledger, Joaquin Phoenix, and even the campy Cesar Romero from the 1960s *Batman* TV series.

What makes the Joker so scary? Joker possesses no superhuman attributes. Instead, he's an expert at chemical warfare, creating gaseous poisons and acid sprays, often emanating from his boutonnière (flower in the buttonhole of his jacket's lapel). In style with his character, he has also used deadly, electrified joy-buzzers when shaking hands with victims, as well as razor-tipped playing cards to be hurled.

The miscreant Joker has had more than one origin story. The most well-known of these is that he began as a thief called the Red Hood. Batman interrupts his $1 million heist, causing him to fall into a vat of chemicals, from which he emerged insane with bleached skin, red lips, green hair, and a perpetual smile on his face.

"They've given many origins of the Joker, how he came to be. That doesn't seem to matter—just how he is now. I never intended to give a reason for his appearance. I thought that . . . it takes away from some of the essential mystery," said cocreator Jerry Robinson, who based the character partly on a joker from a deck of playing cards and partly on a 1920s movie monster name Gwynplaine, whose face was surgically frozen in a smile.[2]

The Joker's real name is Jack Napier, and, like the Voldermort/Harry Potter connection, he killed Bruce Wayne/Batman's parents. "You ever dance with the devil in the pale moonlight?" asks the Jack Nicholson/Joker of all his victims prior to their murders in *Batman* (1989). Death seems to follow the Joker, even in real life. Though Heath Ledger won an Academy Award for his brilliant portrayal of the Clown Prince of Crime in *The Dark Knight* (2008), the actor, who suffered from insomnia and depression, seemed to get even less sleep after deeply immersing himself in the role of the depraved villain. "As you know, madness is like gravity . . . all it takes is a little push," said Ledger as the Joker. That supreme commitment to character might have helped lead to Ledger's untimely demise through an overdose of sleep medication. The movie was released posthumously (after his death) in January 2008.

TIME TO DEBATE

Arguments and debates shouldn't just stop cold. Always offer a conclusion to your position—a clear signal that the end of your argument is coming. Why? A conclusion, much like one you would use to complete an essay, reviews for the listener both your best points and why you believe that your opinion is correct. It allows you to repeat yourself without actually being repetitive, which would waste the listener's time. That's quite a trick, and we recommend using this technique. You can even use several transitional phrases to signal the audience that you are about to conclude your argument. Take notice of how that's achieved below.

Debater #1: "*In conclusion, Lord Voldermort is the absolute G.O.A.T. of Villains. As we have seen he has [repeat your most persuasive argument] . . .*"

Debater #2: "*In summation, Joker is by far the greatest villain of all time because of his . . .*"

LIGHTNING DEBATE

Imagine you're the CEO of a laundry detergent company. Whom would you select to star in your next TV commercial—Batman or Joker? On the surface, it appears they'd both need to get dirt, grime, and even bloodstains out of their clothing/costumes regularly. We'd also love for you to write that commercial for us.

THE ANTIHERO

There are many people who don't root for the hero of a particular story. Rather, they actually pull for the villain, even if only silently to themselves. Why? Sometimes it's easier to relate to the villain. Heroes are often too perfect in their character and seem to represent something unrealistic. Meanwhile, the imperfect villain might be a more relatable character. This perspective gave rise to a new archetypal character—the antihero, a mix of good and evil all rolled into one. Some recognizable antiheroes are *The Simpsons*'s Bart Simpson and gangster boss Tony Soprano from *The Sopranos*.

26

WRESTLER

Mildred Burke vs. Dan Gable

Nearly everyone grows up wrestling—with a baby blanket, your siblings, or kids in the neighborhood. It is one of the natural forms of fun, competition, and self-defense. Wrestling was a significant part of the early Olympic Games, and Homer even mentions it in the *Iliad*, his poetic recounting of the Trojan War. Today, there are many different styles of wrestling, including Folk Wrestling (high school and college wrestling in which the goal is to pin your opponent), Greco-Roman, Freestyle, Sumo (popular in Japan), and professional wrestling. And though the outcomes of many pro wrestling matches were admittedly predetermined, wrestlers such as Hulk Hogan, Dwayne "The Rock" Johnson, and Andre the Giant displayed amazing athleticism in the ring. With wrestling being so diverse, there's little doubt that no matter which two entrants we chose to participate in our debate as the G.O.A.T., you may have someone else in mind. Well, we can always take this hypothetical argument to the mats. Best two out of three falls wins. Ready? Wrestle!

MILDRED BURKE (1915–1989)

On the surface, Mildred Burke, who stood just 5 foot 2 and weighed 138 pounds, didn't appear to be one of the toughest athletes to ever compete in sports. She certainly didn't grow up that way either. It wasn't until she was approximately twenty years old that she saw her first professional wrestling event, which sparked her immediate interest.

Mildred had grown up in extreme poverty. Early in her life, she got a job as a waitress and then as a stenographer (quickly translating someone's spoken words into a system of writing called shorthand). But the idea of wrestling took root in Mildred's mind. She began focusing most of her free time on building muscle and getting stronger. At a local gym, Mildred approached a well-known wrestling promoter, asking that he teach her the sport. The promoter thought it was a joke and a waste of his time, so he told one of the men in the gym to body slam Mildred, hoping to cure her of any more such thoughts. To everyone's shock and surprise, it was Mildred who body slammed that man to the canvass.[1]

Unfortunately, women wrestlers didn't have many opportunities during the 1930s when women's matches were actually banned from many legitimate wrestling events. As a result, to both participate in the sport she felt so passionate about and support herself financially, Mildred Burke began wrestling men at carnivals that traveled across the country. A carnival barker might offer $25 to any man in the audience who could last ten minutes in the ring with Mildred. She wrestled over two hundred men during this time period, losing only once to a college wrestler. The carnival started to bill her as "Mildred Muscles" and "Cyclone Burke."

From her unpublished autobiography, Mildred wrote of her carnival wrestling experience: "I wrestled farmers, mechanics, carpenters, and blacksmiths in a bewildering array of body types and wrestling styles. There was the string bean type, the squat guy who was built like a packing case, and there was the occasional roly-poly. They were pushers, rushers, headlock artists, scissor men, butters, and sluggers. Every single one of them was driven by his own macho thing, and it was vital to all not to be beaten by a young girl in front of their hometown people. Whether they knew anything about wrestling or not, I learned from them all."[2]

Burke worked hard to form a wrestling division for women, eventually starting the World Women's Wrestling Association. Burke herself would become champion and hold her title for nearly two decades.

She trained so hard and was in such tremendous physical condition that the Los Angeles Police Department reportedly put pictures of Burke in their offices to shame male officers who'd gotten flabby and out of shape.

Mildred would hold two other wrestling championships during her career, and helped to promote women's wrestling in other parts of the world including Japan and Australia. She also put her stamp on women's professional wrestling as we know it today by training WWE (World Wrestling Entertainment) Hall of Famer The Fabulous Moolah and former WWE Champion Bertha Faye.

It's hard to imagine, but Mildred Burke, one of the greatest wrestlers of all time, built her career from a single thought before she'd ever set foot inside a wrestling ring: "I can't really tell you why, but I have this feeling inside that I can do it. I want to do it more than anything else in the world. I've been to the matches, and I know I can [wrestle]."[3]

DAN GABLE (B. 1948)

"Once you've wrestled, everything in life is easy." —D. G.

Dan Gable may be the most focused athlete to ever compete in any sport. A huge part of his immense mental stamina is undoubtedly linked to a tragedy Gable suffered as a teen. "[It was] the worst thing that ever happened in my life," said Gable, who at the age of fifteen was away on a fishing trip with his parents when he received word that his nineteen-year-old sister Diane had been discovered stabbed to death in the kitchen of the Gable's Waterloo, Iowa, home. "My sister's death affected my whole life. I dedicated my (wrestling) career and all my accomplishments to her. I said to myself, 'She can't be here with me, but she can look down on me and be proud.' I tried to accomplish much more for her. My dedication to Diane kept me straighter. She was a motivating force. The glory always meant more to me if I knew my parents and my sister would see it."[4]

There are basically two things that have meaning to Dan Gable's life—his family and wrestling. His combined wrestling record in high school and college (at the University of Iowa) was an astounding 181–

1. Gable credits the setback of that lone college loss with making him an even better competitor. "When I'd get tired and want to stop, I'd wonder what my next opponent was doing. I'd wonder if he was still working out. I'd tried to visualize him. When I could see him working, I'd start pushing myself. When I could see him in the shower, I'd push myself harder."[5]

Gable's days were filled with running miles, lifting weights, and grappling on the mats. The injuries have been numerous, including ankles, knees, his neck, ears, and biting through his tongue, lower lip, and cheeks while competing. But he worked through them all. Of course, Gable's body is well tailored to the sport. He has slender hips, powerful wrists, strong sprinter-like legs, and an ability to make his neck disappear like a turtle's, totally frustrating opponents.[6] His incredible combination of talent, desire, and passion are unparalleled in the sport of wrestling.

At the 1972 Olympic Games in Munich, Germany, Gable took the gold medal without surrendering a single point in any of his matches. On the victory stand, in front of the US flag, a limping and bloodied Gable lifted the medal to his lips and kissed it.

"Gold medals aren't really made of gold. They're made of sweat, determination, and a hard-to-find alloy called guts," said Gable.[7]

When Dan Gable's wrestling career was over, he became a wrestling coach at his alma mater, the University of Iowa. Gable's success in coaching has rivaled his success as a competitor. His athletes have won nearly fifty National Championships and a slew of Olympic medals, and Iowa captured an incredible nine consecutive National Wrestling Titles (from 1978 to 1986). A handful of opposing coaches have paid Gable a great compliment by complaining that UI invests too much into their wrestling program's success, and that their schools are at a competitive disadvantage. Only who wouldn't be at a competitive disadvantage when going up against famed wrestler and coach Dan Gable? [8]

TIME TO DEBATE

Now that you've got a handle on how to argue and debate, let's take a look back at some of the vocabulary and techniques we've learned along the way. Every good debater has a "position" or side of the argument in which they believe. This can also be called your "contention" or "resolution." Reasons are vital for convincing others to agree with your position. Those reasons are often referred to as "claims." As the other side tries to poke holes in your reasons, they present what are called "counterclaims." In response to that, you would "refute" or explain why those counterclaims are wrong. A good debater remains relaxed and uses "segues" to link various parts of their argument, keeping a smooth "flow" of ideas. Coming prepared with research on the debate topic is always a smart move. And ending with a conclusion that restates your position and reasons will make a positive impression on the listener.

WHAT'S IN A NAME?

Wrestler Roscoe Monroe (1928–2006), better known as "Sputnik" Monroe, ruled the ring on the Memphis, Tennessee, wrestling circuit from 1950 through the 1960s. How did he get the nickname "Sputnik"? Audiences in the Jim Crow South during this period were segregated, meaning Blacks and whites didn't sit together. Instead, Blacks were forced to sit in the balcony of Memphis's Ellis Auditorium while whites sat in the ringside floor seats, each paying the same price. Monroe, who was white, had enough of this policy and threatened not to wrestle, which would have caused promoters to lose money. Because of his antisegregation stance, a white woman in a crowd of fans called Monroe a "Sputnik," referring to the Soviet Union's satellite *Sputnik*, implying that Monroe was a communist. Monroe embraced the woman's putdown and adopted the nickname. Eventually, the promoters gave in, and the audiences at Ellis Auditorium became desegregated, thanks in part to a wrestler called Sputnik. Singer/songwriter Otis Gibbs has memorialized Monroe's story in a song called *Sputnik Monroe*. Check it out on YouTube.

(27)

WRITER
William Shakespeare vs. Mark Twain

In one way or another, we are all writers. Some of us write homework assignments, shopping lists, e-mails, and texts to our friends and family. Others produce writing that is more story-based, such as novels, short stories, essays, songs, or scripts for TV or movies. Whether your work ever makes it onto a library shelf of not, if you're actively writing, then we consider you to be a writer. Congratulations! But who's the G.O.A.T. of writing? What are the criteria? Is it whose work has been read the most? Whose written words have touched readers in the most profound way? It's extremely hard to say. After all, writing was never meant to be part of any competition. But we'll keep in step with the theme of this book and let you debate our entries in this category.

WILLIAM SHAKESPEARE (1654–1616)

William Shakespeare was an English playwright and poet. More than four hundred years after his death, Shakespeare's work is still an integral part of our society, reflected in our language and entertainment. He is best known for writing plays—comedies and tragedies—which are widely read, and acted out by professionals, amateurs, and students.

Nearly everyone is familiar with his titles *Romeo and Juliet*, *Hamlet*, *Macbeth*, *King Lear*, and *Julius Caesar*. They are stories that touch upon timeless topics such as love, friendship, and revenge. Shakespeare is nicknamed "The Bard," which refers to a poet of the oral tradition (someone whose work is spoken out loud). If you've ever had difficulty reading Shakespeare, it's probably because of the language in which he writes. It's called Elizabethan English, meaning during the reign of England's Queen Elizabeth I (1558–1602). That's important to note. Why? Shakespeare is widely considered one of the greatest writers of all time because of his use of language. He is praised for his ability to choose the right words to evoke feelings in the reader—feelings that make us care about the characters and the outcome of their story. Yet Shakespeare achieves all of that while writing in a language that is no longer spoken. And he does it all in a style called "iambic pentameter" (a line of verse consisting of five metric feet). That's simply amazing!

Shakespeare's most famous stories have been borrowed many times over by modern writers. The plot of *Romeo and Juliet* has inspired *Westside Story*, *Gnome'o & Juliet*, and *Dirty Dancing*. Disney's *The Lion King* is based on *Hamlet*, a story in which the power-hungry uncle attempts to seize control over a kingdom by killing the protagonist's father. The classic sci-fi film *Forbidden Planet* mirrors Shakespeare's play *The Tempest*. The film *She's the Man* owes its premise to the Shakespearean comedy *Twelfth Night*, while the romantic comedy *10 Things I Hate about You* is based on The Bard's *Taming of the Shrew*.[1] Shakespeare is also credited with inventing over three thousand words. They include bedroom, bandit, green-eyed (to describe jealousy), lonely, undress, unreal, and swagger. Now that's a writer with *swag*. Shakespeare coined (invented) the phrases "dogs of war," "heart of gold," "it's Greek to me" (meaning I can't understand it), and "fair play."[2] He also coined the current spelling of the name "Jessica" for his play *The Merchant of Venice*.

MARK TWAIN (B. 1835)

Mark Twain is actually a pen name or pseudonym. The author's real name is Samuel Langhorne Clemens. *Mark Twain* means two fathoms (twelve feet) deep, safe enough for a riverboat not to run aground along the Mississippi River. Twain, who was once a riverboat pilot, often wrote pointed truths about American culture and found himself in deep water because of it. So he chose a rather fitting name under which to write. Shakespeare's stories are about England. Twain writes about life in America. Two of his major works are *The Adventures of Tom Sawyer* and *Adventures of Huckleberry Finn*. The protagonists of those novels are preteens. In a way, Mark Twain invented young adult literature. The author was also interested in science and science fiction. His novel *A Connecticut Yankee in King Arthur's Court* features a protagonist who travels back in time, bringing modern science back to the era of King Arthur in England.

Mark Twain. *Photofest © Photofest.*

Why do comedians Kevin Hart and Dave Chapelle owe Mark Twain a debt of gratitude? Twain was actually the first stand-up comedian. He practically invented the art, traveling across the country and packing theaters where he told humorous stories about people, politics, and American culture.

Today, *Adventures of Huckleberry Finn* is banned by many schools due to its use of the N-word. In case you don't remember, Huck, a ten-year-old boy, heads down the river on a raft with Jim, an escaped slave. After playing a dirty trick on Jim (making him believe Huck was dead), Huck is forced to apologize. Huck states, "It was fifteen minutes before I could work myself up to go and humble myself to a n*****; but I done it, and I [wasn't] ever sorry for it afterwards, neither. I didn't do him no more mean tricks, and I wouldn't [have] done

WRITER'S DELIGHT

When it comes to knowing about great writers, we want you to look like a genius. So here are some facts and trivia that will make you the envy of any librarian.

Poet Emily Dickinson, who preferred the solitude of her own company over that of other people, never intended to be a famous writer. She hid most of her poems in her bedroom, which during her later life, she rarely left. The bulk of her approximately 1,800 groundbreaking poems were found by her younger sister after Dickinson's death.

Maybe you're taking Spanish, French, Italian, or Japanese at school. Perhaps you're doing well in it. But how would you like to write a novel in a language that's not your own? Writer Joseph Conrad grew up in Poland, speaking only Polish. He didn't become fluent in English until he was in his twenties. Considering it was his second language, it's amazing that Conrad penned two of the arguably greatest English-language novels in history—*Heart of Darkness* and *Lord Jim*. The epic war film *Apocalypse Now* is based on Conrad's *Heart of Darkness*.

Did you know the NFL's Baltimore Ravens find their roots in the work of mystery writer and poet Edgar Allan Poe? Poe died in the city of Baltimore and is buried there. His grave is a tourist attraction. Poe's most famous work is his poem "The Raven," in which the ominous talking bird can only say the word, "Nevermore." The Ravens football team is named for Poe's poem.

that one if I'd a [known] it would make him feel that way." Twain purposely chooses to have Huck use that derogatory word to emphasize the fact that this young boy, who wasn't born with prejudices, learned it from the society around him. We warned you that Mark Twain was willing to get himself into deep water.

There are plenty of great writers that we've left out of our G.O.A.T. discussion. They include Toni Morrison, who wrote *The Bluest Eye* and *Beloved*, John Steinbeck (*The Grapes of Wrath*, *Of Mice and Men*, *The Pearl*), Jane Austen (*Pride and Prejudice*), Leo Tolstoy (*War and Peace*), Gabriel Garcia Marquez (*One Hundred Years of Solitude*), and Maya Angelou (*I know Why the Caged Bird Sings*). Ask your English teacher or parents who their choice is for the greatest writer of all time. They'll probably share with you some of their personal favorites. You can also start a classroom discussion or book club in which you might hear some spirited debate on the subject.

FINAL TIME TO DEBATE

Throughout these chapters you may have been asking yourself—exactly who uses these debate and arguing skills in their daily lives? Well, the rather all-encompassing answer is teachers, students, coaches, referees and umpires, salespeople, lawyers, doctors, police officers, judges, journalists, military personnel, reporters, writers, musicians, engineers, technicians of all kinds, and many, many more.

We hope that this book helped you to experience more of the fun and excitement of voicing your own opinion through argument and debate. And that one day in the not-so-distant future, when a group of people gather to argue who's the greatest of all time at something, yours is one of the respected names being debated (perhaps even for the art of debating). Wouldn't that be supercool!

—Paul Volponi

NOTES

CHAPTER I. ATHLETE (ALL AROUND): MILDRED "BABE" DIDRIKSON ZAHARIAS VS. JIM THORPE

1. Don Van Natta Jr., *Wonder Girl: The Magnificent Sporting Life of Babe Didrikson Zaharias* (New York: Little, Brown and Company) (August 18, 2020).
2. Top 25 Quotes by Babe Didrikson Zaharias, Quotes A–Z (November 5, 2020).
3. Top 6 Quotes by Jim Thorpe, Quotes A–Z (December 6, 2020).
4. Victor Mather, "The 100-Year Dispute for Jim Thorpe's Olympic Golds," *New York Times* (December 15, 2020).
5. Top 6 Quotes by Jim Thorpe, Quotes A–Z (December 6, 2020).
6. "Quotes," The Official Licensing Website of Jim Thorpe, cmgww.com (December 15, 2020).

CHAPTER 2. BAND (MUSIC): THE BEATLES VS. ROLLING STONES

1. Paul McCartney Quotes, beatlesquotes.com (August 15, 2020).
2. John Lennon Quotes about Songwriting, A–Z Quotes.com (August 12, 2020).

3. Legacy Staff, "Who Influenced the Rolling Stones?" legacy.com (August 17, 2020).

4. Mick Jagger Quotes, brainyquote.com (August 6, 2020).

5. Keith Richards Quotes, Author of Life, goodreads.com (September 3, 2020).

6. Ibid.

CHAPTER 3. BASEBALL PLAYER: BABE RUTH VS. HANK AARON

1. Babe Ruth, Famous Quotes, bing.com (October 13, 2020).

2. Ibid.

3. Alan Schwarz and John Thorn, "From Babe to Mel: The Top 100 People in Baseball History," in *Total Baseball: The Ultimate Baseball Encyclopedia* (Wilmington, DE: Sport Media Publishing Inc., 2004), 818–820.

4. Ibid.

5. Brian Kachejian, "History of the Baby Ruth Bar and Reggie Bar," https://classicnewyorkhistory.com/history-of-the-baby-ruth-bar-and-reggie -bar/ (March 3, 2020).

CHAPTER 4. BUILDING DESIGNER/ARCHITECT: ZAHA HADID VS. FRANK LLOYD WRIGHT

1. John Zukowsky, "Zaha Hadid: British Architect," britannica.com (August 11, 2020).

2. "Zaha Hadid," azquotes.com (August 1, 2020).

3. "Falling Water," Frank Lloyd Wright, franklloydwright.com (September 6, 2020).

4. Amy Plitt, "Frank Lloyd Wright's Guggenheim Museum: the history of the masterful New York building," nycurbed.com (November 14, 2020).

5. Frank Lloyd Wright Quotes, brainyquote.com (November 14, 2020).

6. Nicholas Ricketts, "Jenga, Jenga, Jenga," Strongmuseum.org (December 1, 2020).

CHAPTER 5. CHESS PLAYER: HOU YIFAN VS. GARRY KASPAROV

1. Alex Palmer, "The Exceptional Genius of Hou Yifan," Espn.com (August 10, 2020).

2. GibChess, "Chess Is a Part of My Life But Not My Whole Life," youtube.com (September 11, 2020).

3. "No 1 Woman and Professor at 26, Loses In Online Return," the *Guardian*, https://www.theguardian.com/sport/2020/jul/17/chess-hou-yifan -no-1-woman-and-a-professor-at-26-makes-uneven-return (August 17, 2020).

4. "Top 25 Quotes by Garry Kasparov," azquotes.com (September 3, 2020).

5. Jan Timman, "The Longest Game," newinches.com (September 3, 2020).

6. Top 25 Quotes by Garry Kasparov, azquotes.com (September 3, 2020).

7. Joshua Keating, "Garry Kasparov: Obama Going to Russia Now Is Dead Wrong," Slate.com (September 4, 2020).

8. Top 25 Quotes by Garry Kasparov, azquotes.com (September 3, 2020).

CHAPTER 6. COMPOSER: JOHN WILLIAMS VS. LUDWIG VAN BEETHOVEN

1. John Williams Quotes, brainyquote.com (May 3, 2020).

2. John Williams' Theme from Jurassic Park: Dino-Tastic, classicalex burnes.com (April 23, 2020).

3. "Interesting Facts about Beethoven," iloveindia.com (August 1, 2020).

4. Ludwig van Beethoven Quotes (Author of Beethoven's Letters), goodreads.com (August 11, 2020).

CHAPTER 7. DANCER (FEMALE), DANCER (MALE): ANNA PAVLOVA VS. JANET JACKSON, MIKHAIL BARYSHNIKOV VS. MICHAEL JACKSON

1. Anna Pavlova, biography.com (September 11, 2020).

2. Anna Pavlova, azquotes.com (September 11, 2020).

3. Judy Mitoma, *Envisioning Dance on Film and Video* (Routledge, 2003), 16 (September 12, 2020).

4. Ibid.

5. Janet Jackson, azquotes.com (September 11, 2020).

6. Mikhail Baryshnikov Quotes, brainyquote.com (September 5, 2020).

7. Soviet Dancer Mikhail Baryshnikov Defects from U.S.S.R., history .com (September 3, 2020).

8. How Michael Jackson Changed Dance History, biography.com (September 1, 2020).

9. Michael Jackson Quotes, goodreads.com (September 1, 2020).

10. Lewis Segal, "Why Michael Jackson Danced Like No One Else," https://latimesblogs.latimes.com/culturemonster/2009/06/michael-jackson -a-dancer-like-no-other.html#:~:text=We%20know%20that%20he%20 tried,That%20was%20his%20triumph (June 26, 2009).

CHAPTER 8. ELECTRIC GUITAR PLAYER: JIMI HENDRIX VS. B. B. KING

1. Michael Kasha, "A New Look at the History of the Classic Guitar," *Guitar Review* (August 1968), 30 (December 2, 2020).
2. Jimi Hendrix, spotify.com (December 5, 2020).
3. 20 Electrifying Jimi Hendrix Quotes, addicted2success.com (December 5, 2020).
4. Eric Clapton on Jimi Hendrix, youtube.com (December 11, 2020).
5. Daniel Silliman, "How the Church Gave BB King the Blues," washingtonpost.com (December 1, 2020).
6. BB King Quotes, brainyquote.com (December 1, 2020).
7. BB King's Playing Style, wordpress.com (December 1, 2020).
8. Guitar Heroes: BB King, marshall.com (December 4, 2020).
9. Why Did BB King Name His Gibson Guitar Lucille? guitarinteractivemagazine.com (December 12, 2020).
10. Prizmi Tripathi, "Robert Messel from AGT: Everything We Know," thecinemaholic.com (December 5, 2020).

CHAPTER 9. HOOPS STAR (FEMALE), HOOPS STAR (MALE): MAYA MOORE VS. ANN MEYERS, LEBRON JAMES VS. MICHAEL JORDAN

1. Maya Moore Quotes, brainyquote.com (December 5, 2020).
2. Ibid.
3. Alana Glass, "How Ann Meyers Drysdale Played like a Girl and Won," forbes.com (December 10, 2020).
4. Ibid.
5. LeBron James, brainyquote.com (December 14, 2020).
6. Ibid.
7. Michael Jordan Quotes (Author of *Driven from Within*), goodreads.com (December 10, 2020).
8. Ibid.

CHAPTER 10. INVENTOR: LEONARDO DA VINCI VS. NIKOLA TESLA

1. Nine Incredible Leonardo da Vinci Inventions, historylists.org (December 18, 2020).

2. Leonardo da Vinci's Armored Car Invention, davinciinventions.com (December 18, 2020).

3. Lauren Kent, "The Nikola Tesla Inventions That Should Have Made the Inventor Famous," https://www.cnn.com/2019/10/25/world/most-famous-tesla-inventions-scn/index.html (October 25, 2019).

4. Nikola Tesla: Biography, Facts & Inventions, britannica.com (December 18, 2020).

5. Ibid.

6. Jeremy Hsu, "Hedy Lamarr: Hollywood's Secret Weapon Inventor," https://www.nbcnews.com/id/wbna46848978 (March 25, 2012).

CHAPTER 11. JAZZ SOLOIST: ELLA FITZGERALD VS. MILES DAVIS

1. Top 25 Quotes by Ella Fitzgerald, azquotes.com (December 12, 2020).

2. Ibid.

3. Fred Kaplan, "Why Miles Davis' Kind of Blue Is So Great," slate.com (December 13, 2020).

4. Miles Davis Quotes, brainyquote.com (December 13, 2020).

5. Ibid.

6. 16 Musicians on the Everlasting Influence of Miles Davis, thefader.com (December 13, 2020).

CHAPTER 12. JOCKEY: ANGEL CORDERO JR. VS. JOHN VELAZQUEZ

1. All work done from personal interviews conducted by Paul Volponi.

CHAPTER 13. MARTIAL ARTIST: RICKSON GRACIE VS. BRUCE LEE

1. Rickson Gracie Biography, imbd.com (December 14, 2020).

2. Rickson Gracie Quotes and Sayings, inspiringquotes.us (December 14, 2020).

3. Is Rickson Gracie Truly the Greatest BJJ Practitioner of All Time? https://www.bjjee.com/articles/is-rickson-gracie-truly-the-greatest-bjj-practitioner-of-all-time/ (December 14, 2019).

4. Rickson Gracie Quotes and Sayings, inspiringquotes.us (December 15, 2020).

5. Bruce Lee Author Quotes, goodreads.com (December 15, 2020).

6. Ibid.

CHAPTER 14. MATHEMATICIAN: SRINIVASA RAMANUJAN VS. SIR ISAAC NEWTON

1. Alane Lim, "Biography of Srinivasa Ramanujan, Mathematical Genius," https://www.thoughtco.com/srinivasa-ramanujan-4571004 (December 26, 2018).

2. G. H. Hardy and Edward M. Wright, *An Introduction to the Theory of Numbers* (Oxford, UK: Oxford University Press 1954), 412 (December 16, 2020).

3. Elizabeth Nix, "Did an Apple Really Fall on Isaac Newton's Head?" history.com (December 17, 2020).

4. Isaac Newton: The Man Who Discovered Gravity, https://www.bbc.co.uk/teach/isaac-newton-the-man-who-discovered-gravity/zh8792p (December 17, 2020).

5. Isaac Newton: Math and Calculus, storyofmathematics.com (December 18, 2020).

CHAPTER 15. MC (HIP-HOP ARTIST): NAS VS. JAY-Z

1. Margaret Jackson, "Nas," oxfordmusiconline.com (December 18, 2020).

2. Nas Quotes, brainyquote.com (December 18, 2020).

3. Emmad Mazhari, "Why Is Nas Thought to Be One of the Greatest Rappers of All Time?" quora.com (December 18, 2020).

4. Jay-Z Quotes, brainyquote.com (December 18, 2020).

5. Anthony Washington, "Hip-hop Head for over 20 Years," quora.com (December 18, 2020).

6. Jay-Z Quotes, brainyquote.com (December 18, 2020).

7. Erik Nielson, "Where Did All the Female Rappers Go?" npr.org (December 18, 2020).

8. Rahel Gebreyes, "Queen Latifah on Fighting Misogyny in Rap and Uplifting Women," huffpost.com (December 18, 2020).

CHAPTER 16. ORATOR (PUBLIC SPEAKER): MARTIN LUTHER KING JR. VS. SIR WINSTON CHURCHILL

1. Winston Churchill: Leadership during WWII, britannica.com, (January 4, 2021).
2. Winston Churchill's Their Finest Hour Speech, poloticmag.net (January 4, 2021).

CHAPTER 17. PHILOSOPHER: PLATO VS. ALBERT CAMUS

1. Plato: Stanford Encyclopedia of Philosophy, stanford.edu (January 5, 2021).
2. Plato Quotes, goodreads.com (January 6, 2021).
3. NS Gill, "An Introduction to Plato and His Philosophical Ideas," thoughtco.com (January 6, 2021).
4. Albert Camus: Biographical, nobleprize.org (January 6, 2021).
5. Albert Camus Quotes, azquotes.com (January 6, 2021).

CHAPTER 18. QUARTERBACK: JOE MONTANA VS. TOM BRADY

1. Joe Montana Quotes, brainyquote.com (February 10, 2021).
2. Ibid.
3. Tom Brady Quotes, brainyquote.com (February 10, 2021).
4. Ibid.

CHAPTER 19. SCIENCE FICTION FRANCHISE: *STAR TREK* VS. *STAR WARS*

1. Gene Roddenberry Quotes, goodreads.com (February 1, 2021).
2. George Lucas Quotes, brainyquote.com (February 1, 2021).
3. Ki Mae Heusner, "Nine Sensational Sci-fi Ideas That Came True," abc news.go.com (February 1, 2021).

CHAPTER 20. SCIENTIST: MARIE CURIE VS. ALBERT EINSTEIN

1. Mark Barna, Gemma Tarlach, and Nathaniel Scharping, "The Ten Greatest Scientists of All Time," discovermagazine.com (February 10, 2021).

2. Marie Curie Quotes, azquotes.com (February 10, 2021).

3. Marie Curie: The Woman Who Stirred Up Science, historyextra.com (February 10, 2021).

4. Albert Einstein Quotes, goodreads.com (February 10, 2021).

5. Relativity, britannica.com (February 11, 2021).

6. From Graduation to the Miracle Year of Scientific Theories, britannica.com (February, 11, 2021).

7. Albert Einstein Quotes, goodreads.com (February 10, 2021).

8. The Kennedy-Nixon Debates, history.com (February 12, 2021).

CHAPTER 21. STUNT PERSON: DAR ROBINSON VS. JEANNIE EPPER

1. The Ultimate Stuntman: A Tribute to Dar Robinson, youtube.com (December 5, 2020).

2. Dar Robinson, Stuntman, Dies, nytimes.com (December 5, 2020).

3. Malcolm Venable, "This 78-Year-Old Stuntwoman Has Defied Expectations (and Death) Her Whole Career," tvguide.com (December 6, 2020).

4. Stuntwoman Jeannie Epper on her proudest career achievement, youtube.com (December 6, 2020).

CHAPTER 22. SUPERHERO SQUAD: JUSTICE LEAGUE VS. AVENGERS

1. John Jackson Miller, "A Brief History of the Justice League—In All Its Incarnations," ew.com (November 1, 2020).

2. Hall of Justice, dcfandom.com (November 1, 2020).

3. Stan Lee and George Mair, *Excelsior! The Amazing Life of Stan Lee* (Fireside Books, 2002), 13 (November 2, 2020).

4. Rick Marshall, "Eight Real Places That Inspired Superhero Headquarters," mentalfloss.com (November 2, 2020).

CHAPTER 23. TV MOMENT: MOON LANDING VS. ELLEN'S COMING-OUT EPISODE

1. James Jeffrey, "Apollo 11: The Greatest Single Broadcast in Television History," bbcnews.com (October 27, 2020).

2. Amy Shira Teitel, "How NASA Broadcast Neil Armstrong Live from the Moon," popsci.com (October 27, 2020).

3. Brian Stelter, "Apollo11: Remembering Walter Cronkite's Words on the Day of the Moon Landing," cnnnews.com (October 27, 2020).

4. Controversial Coming-Out Episode of *Ellen* Airs, history.com (October 28, 2020).

5. How Ellen DeGeneres' Historic Coming-Out Episode Changed Television, biography.com (October 29, 2020).

6. Ellen Celebrates the 20th Anniversary of Her Coming Out Episode, youtube.com (October 28, 2020).

CHAPTER 24. VIDEO GAME: *MARIO BROTHERS* VS. *PAC-MAN*

1. Cesa Games White Papers, Computer Entertainment Supplier's Association, cesa.or.jp (August 18, 2020).

2. Top 25 Quotes by Shigeru Miyamoto, azquotes.com (August 18, 2020).

3. Mark Savage, "The Actors Hiding inside Your Video Games," bbc.com (August 18, 2020).

4. Chris Green, "Pac Man," salon.com (August 18, 2020).

5. Quotes by Toru Iwatani, azquotes.com (August 18, 2020).

CHAPTER 25. VILLAIN (FICTIONAL): LORD VOLDEMORT VS. JOKER

1. Brandon Layne, "What Makes Voldemort a Good Villain?" quora.com (January 19, 2021).

2. Travis Langley and Michael Uslan, *The Joker Psychology: Evil Clowns and the Women Who Love Them* (Sterling, 2019), 180 (January 19, 2021).

CHAPTER 26. WRESTLER: MILDRED BURKE VS. DAN GABLE

1. Mildred Burke, Embarrassing Men and Blazing Trails for Women in Wrestling, prowrestling.com (October 22, 2020).

2. Ibid.

3. Mildred Burke: WWE, wwe.com (October 23, 2020).

4. Iowa Wrestling: Even Early in His Coaching Career Wrestling Icon Admitted That He's One Hell of a Coach, hawkcentral.com (October 24, 2020).

5. Top 25 Quotes by Dan Gable, azquotes.com (October 24, 2020).

6. Wrestling Icon Dan Gable Receives Presidential Medal of Freedom, cbs2iowa.com (December 20, 2020).

7. Top 25 Quotes by Dan Gable, azquotes.com (October 24, 2020).

8. Bio: About Dan Gable, dangable.com (October 25, 2020).

CHAPTER 27. WRITER: WILLIAM SHAKESPEARE VS. MARK TWAIN

1. Mrs. B. Marsh, "Shakespeare Blog: Is Shakespeare Still Relevant to Modern Society," wordpress.com (January 5, 2021).

2. 15 Words Invented by Shakespeare, grammerly.com (January 5, 2021).

INDEX

ABOUT THE AUTHOR

Paul Volponi is an author, educator, and journalist. His twelve novels for young adults have received a dozen American Library Association honors. His novel *Black and White*, winner of the International Reading Association's Children's Book Award, is a staple in many middle school and high school English classes. His novel *The Final Four*, recipient of five-starred reviews, is on the New York City Chancellor's Ninth Grade reading list. Paul is also the author of two nonfiction sports-themed books for Rowman & Littlefield: *That's My Team: The History, Science and Fun behind Sports Teams' Names*, and *Streetball Is Life: Lessons Earned on the Asphalt*. All of his works can be viewed at paulvolponibooks.com.